MW01235649

UNIVERSAL APPEAL

THE BOTTOM LINE

BENEFIT OF DIVERSITY

Ivory Dorsey

KENDALL/HUNT PUBLISHING COMPANY
4050 Westmark Drive   Dubuque, Iowa 52002

Contents

Acknowledgements

I want to first express my thanks to my mother, **Mary L. Wood**. I want to thank her for being the strong woman that she is and for always allowing me to be me. Thank you for being there for me through thick and thin, for always being there to support me. I want to thank you for being my rock, it is because of you that I never felt that I had played my last card—you are my "ace in the hole."

I want to thank all of my **family** for offering unconditional love, humor, and support over the years. For believing in me when many times, I was experiencing doubt.

I want to thank **all of the people** that I have met and have shared different experiences with over the years. This span reaches all over the world, I am sure. I am nothing more than the total composite of all of my experiences. Each of you have played a dynamic role in the personal and professional etching of who I am today. Thank you.

I want to offer special thanks to **Xerox Corporation** for the 10 years I spent there. It was perhaps the 10 most defining years of my professional life. I am thankful for being chosen at such a critical time in the history of the organization. This experience in this great organization, provided me the opportunity for self discovery. I found growth and maturity through all of the perils and all of the pleasures. It was during this corporate experience that I formed my corporate values and found the depth of my personal fortitude.

I want to thank the organization within Xerox, **Minorities United In The Southern Region** (MUSR). These professional pioneers taught me how to navigate through the mine fields of survival. You were my first corporate teacher in Survival 101.

I want to pay tribute to **Julyn Polk,** my first and only African-Female manager, now deceased. Thank you for saying the words that provided the encouragement I needed from day one, *"you can do that job Dorsey!"* I will never forget you.

I want to also pay special tribute to **Gerald Mitchell,** an African-American male manager and colleague at Xerox, also now deceased. Gerald saw the vision and first fed the talent of my potential as a motivational speaker and trainer long before I recognized it as a special gift. He went to his grave planning a motivational rally of which I was to be one of the speakers. Thank you Gerald for your confidence and encouragement, I finally saw it and I am living the vision.

Finally, I want to thank **God.** I truly believe that everything happens for the good of those who love God and are called unto his purpose. It has been good and it is getting better.

Preface

Universal Defined

Including or covering all or a whole collectively or distributively without limit or exception. Comprehensive broad, and versatile. Adapted or adjustable to meet varied requirements.

Appeal Defined

1. Attractiveness

2. Request for reconsideration

In pursuit of blood for health care purposes, there is a unique donor in the ABO blood group called a "universal donor." What makes this donor unique is that his or her blood type is type "O." This means that this person can **donate** blood to any recipient.

There is also another factor called the "universal recipient." This person belongs to ABO blood group and has a blood type called "AB." The person with this blood type can **receive** blood from any donor.

As we progress into this book, I ask you to operate from the definitions stated above. As we look at "universal," we want to examine the totality or the global aspect of the workplace and of the marketplace. We want to examine all of the people in these two areas as we strive to achieve as professionals.

As we look at "appeal" we want to take a two pronged view: (1) The act of being appealing to any recipient and (2) a request for reconsideration of the whole concept of Diversity and its bottom line impact.

I challenge you to suspend everything you feel that you know about Diversity and its impact on the workplace. I ask you to revisit it from this vantage point. It is of particular importance to see yourself and the people that you encounter as both universal donors and universal recipients of skills, ideas, services, revenue, etc.

It is my belief that this is true. Selling and buying are the lifeblood of industry. At one point or another we all are buyers and sellers feeding an economy driven by the heartbeat of needs. As the heartbeat of competitive pressures and customer demands pumps the blood throughout the body of reality, it must do so in a way that is compatible with the existing cells of people and the blood type supporting those cells.

As the world moves more and more toward universal access, the opportunities and the demands will become more and more undefined. Each person will find the need to have universal appeal. In many cases people will be making a universal appeal as they attempt to sell or to buy products from those outside of their respective "comfort zone." The appeal will be for understanding, uplifting, and finally for unity.

It is my belief that America had to go through the process that led us to Diversity. No one can predict what would have happened if certain events had not taken place. We must assume that it was all in order. Because of that order, certain people at different times and places were included and excluded from certain times and places. This includes the "domestic" side of life as well as the "professional" side of life.

Competition, time and technology have become equalizers. The time has come when there really is a place for everyone in every place. For once, it is a true global economy. The boundaries are undefined and in many cases, non-existent. Opportunities are abound. The caveat is that we must find ways to accommodate this new reality and remain whole in the process.

We must suspend our "shoulds" and "ought tos," we must start from where we are, yet we must begin again. The universe has dealt us a powerful hand with many face cards. It is up to us to "play the hand we are dealt."

To the degree that we understand the value of all of the cards and play them at the appropriate time, we will win. Should we choose to discount the value of any card, we will most certainly lose.

We know now that Kenny Rogers was right in the song from "The Gambler" that says:

Every hand is a winning hand, however: you must know when to hold them, you must know when to fold them, you must know when to walk away and when to run. You never count your money when you're sitting at the table, there'll be time enough for counting when the dealing is done.

It is my contention that this is true for us. To the degree that we can amass the information we need from the people that we meet, we can achieve our goals. This will only be done through *Universal Appeal: The Bottom Line Benefit Of Diversity.*

We are already diverse, that is one of the cards. Nothing and no one is going to change that fact. My contention is that we should stop trying to change the cards and play the hand. We must also recognize that the game is already in play. We are now either winning or we are losing. The cards we have are all the cards we are going to get.

I am not suggesting that no harm has been done. I am not attempting to exonerate any group. I am strongly suggesting that it is time to move on. It's time for amnesty on all sides. It is time to play and it is truly time to win, together.

INTRODUCTION

SNAPSHOTS FROM THE LIFE OF A "TWOFER"

Twofer defined: In the arena of Affirmative Action, a twofer is one person in a workplace that actually fits into two protected classes. An example: a person that is black and female could be counted once for being African-American and once for being female.

I feel the need to provide some insight into my background. As you delve into this book, you might be tempted to challenge my right to write it. Many might be tempted to make the erroneous assumption that I have not observed, endured, or even heard of the ills of our society when it comes to the Diversity issue. Many would be wrong.

It is my belief that it is because I *have* observed, endured, and heard of the ills of our society that I am writing this book. I am declaring that it is time for a change. I believe that it is time for a chance. It is time for a chance for universal excellence through Universal Appeal. Two wrongs have never made a right and if we continue to do what we have always done, we will continue to get what we have always gotten. I am fully apprised of what has happened in the past and I am ready to move forward.

Here is a snapshot of my past, the differences, and the decision to move on.

Legs, Bean Pole, 6:00, and Olive Oil

As a child that was usually taller than the other children, I use to fantasize about being short, cute, and round like some of the other petite girls. I knew that I was different as I stood a full head above everyone else but the names: Legs, Bean Pole, 6:00, and Olive Oil to name a few; I think the names made it worse.

One of my fantasies involved being able to reduce my height by surgically removing a few inches from the middle portion of my legs so as to be shorter but not lose the ability to walk. I knew when it was time to line up to take pictures and they said "the tallest in the back," it meant me and the boys. I spent a great deal of time daydreaming about being short.

Growing up in DeQuincy, Louisiana with cousin, Jackie Lee

Fortunately, as I got older, I also got wiser. As I started to travel to other parts of the U.S. and to observe other tall girls who obviously felt the way that I did about being tall, I grew to be repulsed by people who hated being tall. Their dislike for the height was evidenced by the slumping shoulders, flat shoes and obvious self hate. No, that was not me. Being tall could not be that bad.

I decided that being tall wasn't bad, self hate was. I discovered that I loved me and everything that came with me. I started to celebrate the "difference." It's funny because so did everyone else. This was most evident and gratifying when I pledged my sorority in college and the "line" which is usually led by the shortest person, during my pledge period, it was reversed—I led the line. Yes!

Not only did I disband the fantasy of getting shorter, I actually came to love and to appreciate being tall. It is a good thing since the chance of me getting shorter was "slim and none." I learned that being different wasn't bad it was just "different."

WHITE MALES

"Mama, Mama, catch me that little white boy so I can play with him." That was my cry when I saw my first live white boy at around six years of age. The closest I had come to seeing a white boy was Dick and Jane in the school book. I had no access to whites in the early stages of my life as my home town, DeQuincy, Louisiana, was totally segregated racially and no one knew enough or cared enough to want to change it.

My first introduction to integration came as my stepfather transferred to Columbus, Georgia in the U.S. Army. It was totally integrated. By then, I was about twelve years old and I was not moved one way or the other regarding the racial issue. Eventually, we ended up back in segregated DeQuincy until I left for college. I attended an all Black state run university, Southern University in Baton Rouge, Louisiana. This was three years after the march on Washington where Dr. Martin Luther King, Jr. delivered his famous "I Have A Dream" speech. It was also three years after the assassination of President John F. Kennedy. The marches were still going on when I entered college. By the time I graduated from college, significant progress had been made by the courageous Civil Rights warriors.

I said all of that to say that here was a totally neutral "body of intelligence." I harbored no bitterness but I would eventually be faced with the non-choice of neutrality in a world obsessed with "differences." I recognize and honor those who fought for change, I was and am a living example of their success. Segregation was virtually eliminated. Now as an element of change, I would be faced with survival in this new world. Neutrality of thought in an attempt to be included in the totality of activity was now my challenge. I have never been able to make any sense of why people focused on their diferences instead of what they had in common. Particularly since the differences could not be changed.

GROWING UP A "GIRL"

Brothers, Uncles, and Me

For years, I was the only "girl" in a very unique family of grownups. All the children had been born "male" except me. As a middle child, I did not have the luxury of being first born or the baby. So imagine a middle girl in the midst of really "boy boys" and expressive men. Who do you think got "picked on?" Who was the object of the "jokes?" Who was the object of "clandestine plots" to relieve me of my favorite dish by producing harmless lizards at inopportune times? You guessed it—me. Somehow, I don't ever recall any reference to me being female. I never really thought of being female but I knew that I was "different," lovingly different. I never doubted that they loved me and they protected me; even when I felt that I needed no protection because that's what brothers do.

As I entered the workforce, this activity was called "sexism." Thank God, I was already trained and had many causes to recall the strategies to combat "brotherly" attacks. Many times they were not so brotherly—the strategy was the same.

*Left to right: Eric, Clifton, Ivory, Tim,
Mother & Step-father*

GET IN THE BACK

These were the words spoken to me as I started my first "domestic" job as motel maid. I was picked up by the motel owner as he did all of the domestics in the colored neighborhood. Since I was first, I gleefully jumped into the front seat. No one had told me that "colored people" did not sit in the front with white people. Why? I did not understand, however, I obeyed. When I returned home and told my mother about that and a couple of other strange and "nitpicking" incidents, her response was simply: "you don't have to go back." I thank God that my mother did not explain. It would have been the beginning of bitterness.

Because she did not explain, it gave me the chance to formulate my own opinion about "white and black." One of my favorite people was Mr. Tom Robinson, a white grocery store owner in our neighborhood. I use to love to visit his store on the way to school. I never experienced anything but humor and encouragement from him. It is a lasting positive memory.

When I left Mr. Tom Robinson's store, I would go to school. A school that was totally segregated. My favorite teacher was Mrs. Marietta Joshua. She was a powerful black woman and a great teacher. I was just as comfortable with her. Both Mrs. Joshua and Mr. Robinson had the same things in common to me, they both encouraged me to be me. They both expressed joy when I interacted with them. They were both very good at what they did as professionals. I saw them both as role models.

A NOTE, A NOD, AND A SMILE

The greatest difference is the difference that comes when, though you cannot speak the language of an admirer, they find a way to communicate admiration. They take the responsibility of "making up the difference." This was most evident **after** an intense day of training in Virginia. The participants were lined up to commend me on a great session and one by one, I accepted their praise. As the line moved to the end, I noticed a very determined woman of Asian descent focusing intently on me. As she made her way to me, she simply grasped my hand and placed a note into it. She nodded, smiled, and walked away. The note simply read: "You are a great lady." She understood me. She knew that I probably would not understand her. She did not penalize me for not understanding her. She made up for the "difference." What a difference!

SO WHAT IS THE POINT?

The point is that it is the differences that make the difference. It is not our duty to change them or to judge them. It is our privilege to enjoy them. It is a part of life. It is a fact of life. There is so much to be done and so little time to do it in, that we would be remiss to waste time on something that no one can or even want to change.

UNIVERSAL APPEAL

So here I am, three decades later and the jury is in. I am a long way from those naive days in DeQuincy. The world has dealt me the same hand that it has dealt everyone else. I am prepared to play that hand. I have discovered that the world spins on the spindle of economics and if one is to succeed, one must spin with the spindle of economics or be left behind. It is my contention that it is not about tall or short, black or white, or any of the other distinctions used by the non-competitive mind (those minds consumed with things other than the business of succeeding). It is about learning to lead. It is about learning to work with other people regardless of their culture, sexual orientation, race, or any of the other differences.

I have found that at any given point and time, any of the so called differences can be an advantage or a disadvantage depending on time and chance. At some point, each of us will be faced with the power and choice of translucence.

Universal Appeal is the only worthy mission. It opens a smorgasbord of doors and is the pathway to peace, productivity, profit and pride.

As you read this book, I ask you to suspend your current realities. Dull the pain and the pleasure of your current realities and think about our world. Think about you. Think about your DNA and how critical it is for you to make your unique contribution to our world. Think about the legacy you will leave. Then ask yourself this question: Do I want to be an ointment for the pain in this world or do I want to be a part of the pain? If you like pain, well surely you will find other purposes for this book. Otherwise, read on.

Universal Appeal—The Bottom Line Benefit of Diversity is about being an ointment (solutions). It is about taking your God given unique excellence, and like translucent face powder, enhanc-

ing everything and everyone you interface with. It is about encouraging others to be an ointment—to be translucent (an en-
hancement).

Many will say that it is over-simplifying a very complex problem. I say that we have tried complex solutions—now let's try
the obvious. This is the premise. We can not change our differences. We do not want to change our biological differences. We
are different for a great purpose in a greater plan. Since the
differences will not be changed—why not incorporate and celebrate them?

Please take the journey with me to *Universal Appeal—The Bottom Line Benefit of Diversity.*

CHAPTER I

THE DAWNING OF DIVERSITY FOR ME

In 1970, I graduated from Southern University in Baton Rouge, Louisiana. Southern was and is a predominantly black college. In retrospect, it made absolutely no difference to me then, however, now I am grateful for the experience. I left Southern ready to meet the world. As fate would have it, the world met me. This occurred in the form of college recruiters making my first experience in the job market painless. They were recruiting teachers to go north. Since Southern is predominantly black, I suppose they were recruiting black teachers to go north. I was assigned to a predominantly white school.

College photo from Southern University in Baton Rouge, Louisiana

Happily and naively, I accepted my first job in Milwaukee Public Schools as a secondary school teacher in the area of business education at a school called, South Division High. Somehow, it never occurred to me that a northern school would have to go so far south to recruit a black teacher—unless, of course, there were insufficient numbers in the north—naiveté was high.

After being literally shocked at the intensity of the cold weather in Milwaukee, I returned to the south—Houston, Texas where I found the waiting list for teacher jobs to be staggering (reality was setting in).

At this time it occurred to me that I should seek a career other than teaching if I wanted to work any time soon. After a painful search, I found that my best option as a new college grad was secretary at a major oil company. Aside from the janitor, I was the only black in an all white male establishment, plus a white female secretary. While I felt tremendously under-utilized, I had no idea why.

After diligently working as a secretary by day and teaching at the community college at night, I started to grow weary and desirous of a greater challenge only to be offered more secretarial opportunities at higher levels.

Finally, I agreed to take on still another secretarial job at a popular radio station but with higher visibility than the oil company. Once again, I was one of few blacks in a predominantly white male establishment. Here my talents were totally utilized, so much so that when I tendered my resignation and my boss asked me what it would take to keep me, my response was "your job." I meant it. There were two other black professionals there, one black male and one black female.

AN EMERGING PATTERN

Naiveté was fading, I had started to see a pattern but no one ever verbalized the practice of "importing" a minority into a predominantly white establishment. After less than six months, the opportunity knocked and I gained the opportunity to secure a professional training job at Xerox Corporation. To my surprise, there were many blacks in many capacities. They made no secret about the fact that "affirmative action" played a major role in me being hired and every other black that was there. This was not communicated by company officials but by other blacks. In fact, it was a black male sales representative that recruited me.

BLACKS UNITED

Upon arriving, I was greeted by what was called: "BLACKS UNITED IN THE SOUTHERN REGION" (BUSR). This organization was subsequently expanded to include other minorities and the name became "MINORITIES UNITED IN THE SOUTHERN REGION" (MUSR). I was immediately invited to a non-mandatory training meeting of minorities on Saturday. The activity was simply learning to survive as a Black in a predominantly white environment, this was 1974. This would prove to be my second job for an entire decade.

We discussed this thing called Equal Opportunity and Affirmative Action and the fact that they were government imposed programs that got us into the organization. However, it was made clear survival was our responsibility. It was made clear that we would be held accountable by our ability to adjust to corporate culture. It was clear that this was white male territory and the culture was *white male* grounded. If one hoped to survive (s)he had to figure out a way to mimic that behavior. One had to mimic that behavior while "over achieving." We learned that "mavericks" were "massacred."

HAD TO BE MORE THAN GOOD

I was in awe. I had grown up in a small southern town and was educated in an all black college. I had witnessed the separation of water fountains and bathrooms by signs that simply said "white" or "colored". It was a far-fetched dream to be working for one of the finest companies in the world, in one of the most visible and critical jobs they had. Xerox truly embraced Equal Opportunity and Affirmative Action policies in word as well as in deed.

Yet I was listening to experienced Blacks telling me that I had to be more than good, I had to be great. I had to be flexible, I had to adapt. I felt it was a small price to pay. I was not suspicious of any "ceiling." I was sensitive only to the fact that white males made the rules and that they had to be learned and skillfully followed. It was the first rule of survival.

WHITE MALE WAS KING

I listened, I asked questions, I played the game. Some I won, some I lost. One thing was always evident—the white male was king. It was his jungle and if I was to survive, I needed to learn the rules and play the game. I learned, I played, I survived. I think. . . .

MOMENT OF TRUTH

After completing 10 years of extraordinary performance in a combination of positions including: customer education, region program management, field sales, field sales management, retail store general management, etc. I decided to try my wings outside of the "nest" or the corporate structure.

They had created an Eagle; I knew how good I was and was yearning to prove it by my own rules. It was my time to soar. This was 1984. I entered the world of consulting—training in the areas I had so painfully learned. My client base is the one I know best—corporations, teaching others how to manage the skills of performance and *survival in a competitive world* without regard for race and gender; there is no time for that. (Little did I know that in the 1990's this would be the mandate for everyone.)

EMERGENCE OF "DIVERSITY"

My mission is to go into major corporations and, as one of my clients once called it, "spread the corporate gospel." "PERFORMANCE, WITHOUT REGARD FOR RACE, GENDER or ANY OTHER SELF DEFINING CHARACTERISTIC IS KING". As a consultant, I see many people, companies, and occurrences. The words of AFFIRMATIVE ACTION AND EQUAL OPPORTUNITY are downplayed and a new word: DIVERSITY has emerged. Some people feel that it is a watered down version of EEO/AA. They are incorrect. EEO/AA is a government mandate. DIVERSITY is a leadership mandate.

Yes, along with everything else. "DIVERSITY" has emerged. I have taught this course for several years and I am still responding to requests to speak on the topic. As a product of EEO/AA and a witness to the emergence of DIVERSITY, it is my contention that though the intent is different and the penalty for failure is much, much greater, the impact is virtually similar—it is an unnatural response. We are still trying to convince people to practice teamwork with the existing team. Many are still resisting.

NEW MINORITIES

In addition to Blacks and other minorities, there is the white female. The rules have been learned, the game is being played. Many are crying "foul". Someone is winning—who is winning, I do not know. From my observation as an external consultant, it appears that each group has an unfair disadvantage. The reason is because no one is free to totally respond to competence driven challenges. The challenge is still to (1) respond to what you are hired to do and (2) manage the reaction to the perceived "differences". In many cases you are wearing two hats and literally speaking two languages.

White males feel that they are being blamed for all of the woes of women and minorities. Many feel that there are "ills" in the workplace related to Diversity, women and minorities feel that the white male is the cause. It is perceived that many minorities and women are contributing to what is called "white male bashing". This leaves the white male in a defensive posture—defending his right to exist in the workplace that he in fact, created.

Women feel that they are not respected as women and many feel that the majority of their ideas are challenged or defeated simply because of the sexist expectations of men. Many believe that there is some mystical secret that keep women from rising as high as they can in their careers. This has been described as the "invisible or glass ceiling". From my viewpoint, I found it to be very visible but subtle. The effect was "playing hardball with a softball mentality." The casualties are great and the real battle is being ignored and lost by default.

MINORITIES: UNFORMIDABLE CONTENDERS

Minorities, both men and women, **believe** that there are a whole set of rules that never get shared with minorities. Many feel that to even be accepted, minorities must be several times better than non-minorities and even with the added expectations, minorities are never seen as equal contenders.

MINORITIES: SUBSET OF SUSPICION

Many minorities experience still another challenge. The added challenge is competition between minorities. Some minority males are perceived by minority females as having more of an advantage because they are male.

Some minority females are perceived by minority males as having an advantage because they classify as two minorities in one by EEO/AA standards, thereby constituting a "twofer" (two minorities in one).

As a result of the subset, the so called built in comfort of allegiance because of similar minority status becomes a subset of suspicion, or value added competition.

THE SCRAMBLE IS ON

And so the scramble is on. *Everyone and no one ignoring the possibility of anyone.* Translated: everyone is being unproductive because they are focusing on revenue deterrents instead of revenue enhancements.

No one is accepting responsibility to resolve the issue by holding themselves accountable. No one is recognizing that anyone can fix the problem by understanding "the power of one" right where they are. This reality is a very sad situation.

AMERICA: THE NEW MINORITY

The reality is that because of all of the infighting in the American workplace, Americans are, through our behavior, rapidly positioning the country to be the "New Minority" in a global economy.

As a country, we have even had discussions about introducing "quota" bills in the Senate and the House. Isn't this the "Q" word that white males found so repulsive when introduced by EEO/AA to give minorities an "equal opportunity"? Much of the conversation I hear today regarding the country actually remind me of the conversations I witnessed as people talked about minorities and their demand for "equality." Now America is talking about it.

It is my contention that the focus on DIVERSITY is not the only solution, common sense is. Instead of focusing on managing diversity, as a country, we should *waste no more time on those things we cannot change and redirect our efforts to things we can do something about.* We are all in the foxhole together whether we like it or not. Never has there been a time when the cliché: **"together we stand, divided we fall"** been more appropriate.

MANDATING EMERGENCE

Instead of "Managing Diversity," America needs to start "Mandating Emergence" and holding everyone responsible and accountable for the process. We need to immerse all of the talent, commitment, and results we can muster and thrust it all toward the onslaught of crumbling of American companies. We witnessed the crumbling of the Berlin Wall, and if we are not careful, Berlin will witness the crumbling of America. It will not be the crashing of the "glass ceiling" but the crashing of dreams as together, we will face massive unemployment through continuing layoffs.

LOST SIGHT OF WHITE MALE EXCELLENCE

We have all been so busy trying to ensure that the white male is not in control, we have forgotten that "control" is something the white male understands very well. Right now, we need more of it. We all need to understand the psyche of this. We have all lost sight of the fact that what the white male had in place was not only good, it was excellent.

When the country was run by white males without all of the distractions, America was on top and lending a helping hand to other countries. We were the model. Because of the resistance to diverse groups showing up for a slice of the action, we are now fighting an internal battle. As a result, we are modeling other countries. As the world moves more globally, China, Vietnam, and other countries are emerging as the place to market and to sell. America is on the list but it is not first on the list. We are talking about getting in on the action also.

MISTAKE OF THE WHITE MALE

White is Right—Only Males Need Apply

If the white male made any mistake at all, it was the mistaken assumption that only "white" was right and only "males" need apply. Women and minorities are declaring that "that dog won't hunt". Not anymore it won't. Technology has diminished the need for brute strength—now, only brain power is a factor. Women have never been accused of "not thinking." Minorities had to think just to live in many cases. So there is no reason to exclude these team members. We need everyone and everyone needs everyone.

From my vantage point, with the exception of one weakness, there were no real problems with the white male process. It was a good process during a time when a process was needed and none existed. *I contend that the only problem was the process of processing others into the process.* There was no deliberate plan or strategy to include others who were not white male. Many white males did not and do not believe that there is a place for others who are unlike themselves. Many continue to fight to maintain the status quo. Therein lies the struggle. Times that were will be no more and everyone must be included.

While *many* white males practice the policy of inclusion, *many* practice the policy of exclusion. Some white males have never really understood the cliché of "what's good for the gander is good for the goose." Until that fact is recognized and respected, we will all continue to be "held hostage." Is this the equal opportunity we want? I don't think so. If we are all held hostage in America, whose minding the store of market share? The answer is evident. We are losing it daily.

WOMEN FIGHTING AN UNNECESSARY BATTLE

Women: What did you have in your hand and had to "let go" to chip at the glass ceiling and where is it now? Who will pay the price for the results of letting go? Is it necessary to chip at the glass ceiling with one hand and fight for your rights with the other?

As long as women have sole power to deliver children, they will have a predominant desire and maternal instinct to lead them by the "hand." In the face of technology, economics, and sheer ambition, today that hand must be released to pursue a tough battle for equality. The battle of preserving the hand in the workplace while maintaining balance at home is a tough battle for one person. This is particularly tough if that battle is unnecessary.

There is one hand in the home and one in the workplace. The one at home is critical to the survival of our country. It has been said that "the hand that rocks the cradle, rules the world." I believe that this is true. When this hand is released, without someone taking hold, it hurts men and women, black and white; it tears at the fabric of our nation. It destroys the family. We need to come together at home and at work for the sake of our children. We need to come together for ourselves, for this nation, and for this world. We have a responsibility to repopulate the world with productive citizens. This starts at home first; it is a shared responsibility.

Today, we are building more prisons than schools. Children are seeking thrills by the number of kills. Ethics, integrity, character, and all of the foundation of life discussions that are home-based responsibilities are being taught on television and on the streets. Raising a family and building a workplace is for everyone. We are everyone and we need to be everywhere. No one should be forced to prove that anymore. We don't have time anymore.

WOMEN AND THE GLASS CEILING

It takes everything you have to chip at the "glass ceiling" because of resistance. The glass ceiling is nothing more that "the thought processes of those in strategic positions that says certain people should not and will not rise above a certain level and they do everything within their power to ensure it." This thought process will and should be resisted by women because women are competent and deserving of demonstrating that competence. If it takes letting go of certain things to gain that right—then so be it. But we all suffer. Men, women, and society. There are no winners in this fight.

PSYCHOLOGICAL WARFARE

Women and minorities recognize that there is resistance. As a result of this resistance, competent minorities and women are forced to work in an environment that is hostile. They work with the constant knowledge that their right to be there is being challenged on a daily basis. The challenge is that you must work to prove them wrong while doing what you are hired to do. It is a seven day a week, 24 hour a day battle. It wrecks nerves, creates nightmares, produces cold sweats in the middle of the night. It creates blindness to your personal surroundings. It creates paranoia, cynicism, and blatant distrust. It creates irritable "parents" who must go home to confused children.

All of these are inconducive to productivity. Little "glass ceiling" battles are fought and won in the internal workplace. Total wars are being lost in the external competitive arena. There is no reason for it. These thought processes must change. Men have contributions unique to men and women have contributions that are unique to women. Society says that there is a place for us all. This is the same message of DIVERSITY.

As long as we are serving a heterogeneous customer base, we need the unique contributions of both men and women, minority and non-minority. We must mirror our customer and our competitive base. It is not homogeneous. We can not afford to fight this battle anymore. It is a lose-lose situation.

PRICE TOO HIGH—THROW IN THE "WHITE MALE" TOWEL—WE MUST THROW IN ALL OF THE TOWELS

We cannot afford this battle for power in the workplace anymore. It is time to throw in the "white" towel and start talking. *Male, female, lesbian, gay, people with disabilities, and other unique categories;* we must start talking about the differences in **strength** and the best way to allocate those strengths of differences to achieve the common mission of victory—our children and our country are depending on it.

As I look at the state of our nation and our world, I recognize that the time for internal fighting is over. I am clear that we have bigger fish to fry. I hope that you feel the same way too.

CHAPTER II

THE DILEMMA OF DIVERSITY

It doesn't matter how you are packaged, we are all the same in the heart.

Oprah Winfrey, ABC News Interview
November 28, 1993

While I consider myself to be somewhat talented at expressing myself both verbally and through the written word, this book is by far, the most difficult challenge for me to write. It is difficult because it requires suspending reality. It requires taking hold and letting go. It requires balancing rage and respect. It requires putting onto paper a continuous form of inner conflict.

As a professional woman who happens to be black, I find myself singing two songs of spiritual origin: *Amazing Grace* and *You Can Make It.* One implies that I have made it already and I am looking back in amazement. The other implies that I am still trying. Both are true. I remember an old song by Mary Wells called, "Two Lovers." In the song, one man brought her joy and the other brought her pain. She describes the two lovers as the same person with a split personality.

This is how I feel as I respond to questions regarding whites and males. As I look back at the trials, tribulations, and successes in my life, I see many people. I see both male and female, black and white. While I must admit that when it came to receiving hell, I received hell from all—I have also given hell to all. To that regard, I received and delivered equal opportunity hell. In this regard, I see myself as just "Ivory." I am not for the fainthearted. The sheer force of my personality would either magnetize you to me or send you into a fit of rage. It brings to me both perils and pleasures.

I once had a fellow officer (white female) of a volunteer association express such strong distaste for me that I finally had to ask her why. I was sure that it had something to do with my color since we were both women. Her response was *"I hate your motivating self-promotional style."* I had to respect what she said because I do have a motivating self-promotional style. She read me well. Since she *did not* have a motivating self-promotional style, I did not bother to thank her for the compliment as left-handed as it was.

The truth was that while generally I liked her as a person, I hated her pessimistic attitude and her resentment for people who would dare risk self promotion. I thought she had a vicious mean streak and would strike at any moment. I felt that she was beyond conversion but was very clear about what she liked and what she did not like. Aside from my style, I don't know if she liked me or not. I guess it doesn't matter since I am never far from my style.

The beauty of the statement was that she separated my style from my body. In addition to isolating me from what she did not like, it enabled me to examine her dislike to determine if I wanted to change it—I did not. My choice was clear—limit my exposure to her.

On the other hand, most of the feedback I get identifies my style as my asset. Generally, I received uncompromising encouragement and support from other African-Americans both male and female; it has contributed greatly to my salvation. Recently, I received a letter from a very accomplished white male commending me on a very challenging presentation. In the letter he said: *"The strongest part of the program is you. Be Ivory."* During the same week I received a letter from a white male professor at a leading university in Atlanta requesting my participation in an upcoming program. In the request, he noted that he had observed me in a prior performance. He stated: I am inviting you to participate on our program because *"I liked your style."*

I am proud to say that the majority of the feedback that I receive regarding my style is similar to the two white males quoted, so why would I give credence to someone so obviously determined to break my spirit? I don't think she liked herself very much—why would I give her dominion over me? I have found that when people are unhappy with themselves, they will be unhappy with everything in their path. I refuse to bear that cross.

The greatest pain experienced is the pain that I have received solely because I was black and/or female. There is something humiliating about that because it leaves you hopeless in your choices. I have always loved the fact that I was black and a woman. I consider myself to be one of God's favorites because I love me just the way I am. (I *even* grew to love my height. It was a source of conflict during my childhood.) So when someone attempts to penalize me because of my very existence, it hurts. It is also in conflict with my motivational style. The choice is to defend or to ignore—neither is a pleasant choice since it dampens the spirit.

Making decisions about other people solely or largely on the basis of their skin color or shape of their eyes or texture of their hair is the defining behavior of one of the most pernicious of the isms: racism. pg. 16
Dr. B. Eugene Griessman
DIVERSITY: Challenges and Opportunities

I have come to pity those who cannot look past the external features of people because it reveals a gross under-development of the realities of their own lives. Had I not come to the realization that the best part of people are the unseen qualities demonstrated by what they produce for others, I would be suicidal by now. I have over the years watched my external qualities go from "hot pants" to "full cut long jeans." It was not to keep warm. In essence, I went from revealing flesh to concealing flesh.

I can recall as a teen, after passing the "straight up and down" phase (being tall and skinny), discovering the smoothness of my skin and the suppleness of my muscles. The limitless energy and all of the external qualities of youth were present. As I grew older and father time started to take his toll, I started to notice that these things are only temporary, they are fading daily!

These strong and attractive body parts are designed to carry you through the trials of life to learn life's lessons. They are designed to give you the power to "trap" experience. I learned that the price of experience is "youth." All of the smooth skin seems to be exchanging places with what looks like chocolate cottage cheese. The muscles, well sometimes they are supple and sometimes they are not. The energy—there is a limit to what I can do and how long I can do it. The bottom line is, the external parts are just that—external. They are simply hardware (body) to process the software (mind).

The only thing that seems to be getting stronger and better is my mind. My ability to reason. My insight and my instincts. I think they call it wisdom and understanding.

I feel good. Every time I think about where I am, where I came from and where I am going, I feel good. I have few doubts about my abilities or my place in the world. I have been given the gift to help others. The gift to help to remove or to still the doubts of others. I have found that I have a true God given gift, a charge to keep. I have found that my time on this earth is limited. I have become more consumed with what I can contribute rather that what I can consume.

I have discovered that we are all just clay, always under construction by an even greater potter. Whether we choose to take part in the construction or not, the construction goes on for better or for worse. I have discovered that this is true for everyone. Mother nature is an equal opportunity force.

It does not matter what color you are, what sex you are, or anything else. If you were born a living thing, be it animal, mammal, plant, bird, or human—this is true for you. The Diversity of Life is without lines. We will all experience the same perils and the same pleasures. Time and chance will happen to us all.

So why the line between the differences? It really does not make a lot of sense. In addition to not making sense, discrimination limits your enjoyment in life. People are always stunned at the intensity of my laughter. They are also probably amused that I find humor in little things, mostly the truth. But I am absolutely happy to be alive. I love the life I live and live the life I love.

I thank God that through all of the perils and pleasures of life, I can still laugh and mean it. I thank God that I can walk into any group, white, black, old and young and feel at ease. Better than that, others who are different from me feel at ease when I am around. We can talk about anything and everything and not feel offended or defensive. I call this, universal appeal.

Yes, I still encounter people who are not comfortable with themselves and as a result, they attempt to make others uncomfortable, including me. But is that my problem? I don't think so. I pity them. I shudder when I think that they will have input into anything regarding opportunities for me. However, I live by the Serenity prayer:

God give me the serenity to accept the things I cannot change, the courage to change the things I can, and the wisdom to know the difference.

There is a book written by Ellis Cose entitled, *The Rage of the Privileged Class.* In it Mr. Cose talks of the rage that exists in the successful black professional. I concur with all that Mr. Cose has reported. However, I must expand upon his findings. I find my greatest challenge to be reconciling the "rage and respect." For every white or male I have encountered that challenged my right to exist because of my sex or my race, I have found countless others who celebrated my courage, my wisdom, my personal power. They became coaches, cheerleaders, and mentors. Many became my friends. They are some of the richest friendships in my life.

I can clearly say that for every time I have been denied an opportunity for racial or sexual reasons, I have been given access to opportunities of greater magnitude. My greatest challenge is knowing when to relax. Oh how I would love to walk around and just be good without being classified as a good black or a good woman. Any attempts to do so are usually doused with "chocolate praise."

I can recall as a professional at Xerox Corporation, I made the decision to enter field sales. I literally withdrew my name from a confirmed secure management position to do so. My mission was to prove once and for all that I could perform in any capacity and against all odds. I wanted to prove that my performance had nothing to do with being black or female. I was ready to shake the "twofer" designation that was elevated every time I received a promotion. I wanted to prove that I was good without condition.

So I went into field sales. I was given the most challenging assignment in the branch. They told me it would be a challenge and that is why they wanted me to handle it. I was honored. It had never been held by a black or a female. It was in Dallas, Texas. It was in the city and the county of Dallas. It was during the most competitive time in the history of Xerox. I recall meeting only one black decision maker the entire time I was responsible for the territory. I was to come face to face with discrimination. Not external from the customers, but internal from a white male.

I was told that the territory had been vacated by several white males who had done a survey to prove that there was no new business in the territory. To be fair, Xerox offered to protect my income for 120 days at 100% to avoid financial ruin. My mission was to protect the "installed" copier population.

A white male, the Government National Accounts Manager was enraged that I was going into the territory. He said that the city and the county of Dallas was not ready for a woman, a black, and it surely was not ready for Ivory Dorsey. He attempted to lobby the other government representatives to keep me out of the territory. He attempted to "protect" the customers from me by appealing to them to bypass me. He would eventually write his own pink slip. He was not acting in the best interest of the company or himself.

He was unsuccessful on many counts. In addition to being wrong about me, the city, and the county; it was a white male who expressed support for me and my ability to meet the challenge. He ensured me that he could not fight the battle for me but that if it got to be too much, he would intervene on my behalf.

I received unlimited support and encouragement from the Xerox leadership team. And while selling in the territory was truly a challenge, it had nothing to do with me. As I look back, this happened to be the most competitive time in the history of the corporation. Until this era, Xerox literally had no competition. The clients were simply exercising the power of choice. The order-taker era was over, it was time to sell.

And sell I did. I established a new level of performance and seldom fell below 300%. The last month in the territory before leaving Dallas, Texas, I was 1229% of plan. I can recall getting my results after moving to Atlanta and calling the Branch Sales Manager in Dallas because they did not include 12 sorter points. He laughed at the fact that with such a high level of performance that I would concern myself with 12 points.

LEADERSHIP WAS A CRITICAL FACTOR

It was an extraordinary period in my life, I felt good about myself, I felt like a contributor. Fortunately, at that time and place, I had good leadership at Xerox. In the book *The Leadership Challenge*, by Kouzes and Posner, they talk about the difference between leaders and managers. Their answer to that question is that,

> *. . . leaders bring out the best in us. They get us to achieve even more than we originally believed possible ourselves. Their belief creates a self-fulfilling prophecy—we do as we are expected to do. . . .The leader's expectations have their strongest and most powerful influence in times of uncertainty and turbulence.*

I found this to be a reality during this time of uncertainty and turbulence. Ron Shamlaty as Branch Manager, and Marnie Milligen as Sales Manager were larger than life for me during this time. Though they were both white, they saw in me the solution to a major challenge. They saw the talent and the desire to succeed, they allowed me to exercise the excellence that I had been building for years. Of all of the challenges I faced, I never once questioned their belief in me. This was a defining period of time in my life. Failure was not an opinion.

I often wonder what kind of performance would I have had if I did not have to fight the internal battle from the Government National Account Representative? What would have happened if it had been someone other than me taking on this challenge; someone not so determined? What would have happened to all of that potential? (By the way, he received no support for his point of view and ended up leaving the company.)

PEOPLE DO NOT BUY FROM COMPANIES, THEY BUY FROM PEOPLE

I learned that people did not buy from companies, they buy from people. I established a wonderful relationship with my clients. And while, they were not accustomed to seeing a black female sales representative, at least not with Xerox, they respected Xerox' decision to send me and we did business. We did a lot of business—more than at any time in the history of that branch.

The relationships were so strong that one retired decision maker, after being told by her son over 14 years later that I was in Atlanta, actually looked me up and we spent the day together. She introduced me to her family and her new grandson. We talked about old times. She recalled that I was on the *"front-end of all that integration."* Fourteen years after I left the territory, ten years after leaving Xerox; and after she retired from the County of Dallas, we still liked and respected each other. It is not about color or gender, it is about people, pride, performance, and professionalism.

EVIDENTLY, THE FAT LADY HAS NOT SUNG

Despite all of my successes, it is not over. I still encounter discrimination and I am still surprised when it happens. I work to not expect it. That would be stereotypical. It is almost as if as soon as I forget that I am black or female, someone decides to "snap me back into reality." It is clearly a heavy burden. I often wonder what and where would I be if people would just see my capabilities. Even as an entrepreneur, I face unspoken discomfort in some areas and total embracing in others. I watch people struggle with personally accepting me and my capabilities but being unsure of being able to sell my color or gender to others. The inner conflict continues. Dr. B. Eugene Griessman, in his book *Diversity: Challenges and Opportunities*, described this scenario quite accurately. He said:

Prejudice does not necessarily lead to overt action. He gives four categories of which number three is the "Unprejudiced discriminators." These are individuals who hold no negative attitudes toward individuals of a particular group and may even like them, but discriminates against them. An example is a fraternity officer who holds no negative attitudes toward Asians, but refuses to support an Asian pledge out of fear that he will lose status in the fraternity. pg 17

I can recall recently receiving a note from a fellow speaker after hearing me speak. It was a very encouraging note that read: *"you get better and better every year. And not because of your color, you have substance. You should be a talk show host."* I wondered if she would say that to anyone but me. I wondered if when asked to recommend someone for a visible position, would she recommend me. I wonder. . . .

I wonder if we will ever get to the point where we will not be a respecter of persons but of deeds, contributions, and talents. I wonder if we will ever operate from the heart.

NOT ONLY UP TO WHITE AND MALES

We must. We must. We must.

One of my most fascinating experiences came when I visited Washington for the first time. I visited the "Tomb of the Unknown Soldier." I watched the guards as they diligently strutted with precision. It was particularly exciting when the "change" took place.

While no one knows who resides in the tomb, everyone knows of the importance of the mission they were protecting when they became a part of the tomb. The guards change but the contents of the tomb and the mission is the same.

In a way, this is where we are as a country. While all of the guards in 1974 were male, I suppose that there are probably some females guarding the tomb now. I am certain that the instructions are the same and certainly the change will be male to male, black to white, male to female, etc. The tomb doesn't care. The mission is still the same though the guards will continue to change. There is a changing of the guard going on in our country and we too must have a seamless transition. We must blur the line between the difference for the good of the overall mission.

The back drop of Diversity is the white male since the white male is the center of Diversity. The very use of the word Diversity means different. In this case, it means different from the white male. However, it is not only a white male problem. We must all pick up the mantle of leadership and move on. We must make a commitment to trust and to try. It is a decision that I have already implemented. My life is enriched by it.

THE TRANSLUCENT MESSENGER/RECEIVER

It is my belief that Universal Appeal is the most powerful appeal there is. We must learn to be translucent. Even the FBI seek agents who can blend in and become a part of the environment. And whereas I am not suggesting that we alter our identity or destroy our uniqueness, I am suggesting that we work harder at becoming mentally compatible. To seek ways to include instead of exclude. To seek common ground on all fronts.

Author Tom McGuane talks about rivers and the power of rivers to humanize and to heal. He says that there isn't anything that a good river could not help. Water is known for its oblivious nature. It will conform to anything, you need only create a pathway. It is a receiver and a sender. Unless altered, it is translucent. It is time for us to become water to a society whose creativity is drying up. There are a number of major rivers and they flow and join together to supply the water needs of society. Without water, there would be no society. Without teamwork there will be no society.

BIGGER FISH TO FRY

Even the rivers are under threat of contamination. The greed, the complacency, and the feeling that *"there is more where that came from"* is taking over. There is no more water and there aren't any more customers. We must change the way we are doing things, the way we think about each other. We must do this to ensure longevity for us and for those who will come after us. This is a senseless battle.

For those who are coming after us, this is a major crisis in itself. In addition to the need to build and to develop the people on our existing teams, we must ensure that the children of this era live to take our places. While we are still struggling with the old battles, new ones are cropping up in the form of drugs, violence, gangs, and crime. We truly must move on, there are bigger fish to fry.

Ellis Cose, in the November 15, 1993 issue of *Newsweek Magazine* segment, *Rage of the Privileged* book excerpt concedes and I concur:

> *It may very well be that the civil rights debate has been so distorted by strategies designed to engender guilt that many whites, as a form of self defense, have come to define any act of decency toward blacks as an act of expiation.*

> *If an end to such strategies—and indeed an end to white guilt—would result in a more intelligent dialogue, I, for one, am all for wiping the slate clean.*

> *Let us decide, from here on out, that no one need feel guilty about the sins of the past. The problem is certainly not that people do not feel guilty enough; it is that so many are in denial. And avoidance is not a good substitute for changing that reality. Nor, more to the point, will it do much to narrow the huge chasm that separates so many whites from blacks.*

I am in total agreement with this observation. It is time to move on, now. We must use all of our resources to maximize what is here while preserving and perpetuating growth simultaneously. The best way to do this is through working together. One team, one cause, many brains.

Dr. Eugene Griessman in his book, *Diversity: Challenges and Opportunities*, levels Diversity with Leadership. He says:

Leadership involves having the vision to see how much can be accomplished if the potential of everyone in the group is fully realized. pg. 54

I naturally seek Diversity in all that I do because it makes sense. Balance always makes sense. In addition, I have acquired a taste for Diversity. I challenge all who will read this book to make a first step today. Blur the line. Start with your neighbors, friends, and colleagues of diverse backgrounds, etc. Create a climate for open dialogue. Do it today.

QUESTIONS ABOUT THIS CHAPTER

1. What is your initial reaction to the foregoing?

2. Does it compare to what you have experienced?

3. What have you observed in the workplace that would contradict or confirm the foregoing?

4. What would you add to the chapter you have just read?

5. What do you see as potential solutions?

Recommendation: Choose a person or a group of persons of different gender, culture, race, etc. and initiate a discussion with the intent being:

1. Enlightenment.

2. Developing a functional action plan personally.

3. Exploring the possibilities of developing a functional action plan for the immediate work area.

CHAPTER III

WHY THE INTERNAL STRUGGLE MUST END

I don't think there are any informed professionals who would deny that there is an internal struggle going on in the general workplace. I call this struggle the "Diversity Equation." I choose not to elaborate on that point right now, I want to make a case for why the internal struggle must end.

I could sum it up in one sentence. "A house divided against itself cannot stand." A more basic reason: competitive effectiveness. Competition always hits where the vulnerability is greatest. Vulnerability is reduced only through a total team effort. Anyone that is inside of the organization is on the team—period.

COMPETITION AND THE BOTTOM LINE

I didn't have to knock this man out. I just had to do a little bit more than him, and that's what I did.
Evander Holyfield
after regaining his title
from Riddick Bowe

There is absolutely no reason to talk about Diversity or any other business strategy unless we talk about it as it relates to competition and the bottom line. Without competition, we could all observe the market, develop our products and services, set our prices and wait. Yes, I said wait. Because if we first observed the market, then we know that there is a need and where there is a need, eventually someone will seek to satisfy that need. Now if no one has a solution to the satisfaction of that need but you, then this means that you have no competitors. In that case, don't worry—be happy. That is not the case for the predominance of businesses in the world.

"A house divided against itself cannot stand."

Competition is usually fierce and heavy. Our competitors are our customers saviours. Competition is an equalizer in that it keeps us thinking, planning, and acting in the best interest of our customers for fear of losing them to our competitors. Our competitors thrive and survive on our mistakes—their only success is our failure. In many cases we are just one flicker of a "switch" away from competitive intrusion. At the time of intrusion, we must have a competitive response or risk being overtaken.

The health of your bottom line depends on the ability to keep competition out of your customer base. The ability to keep competition out of your marketshare depends on a combination of quality of products and services, competitive pricing, and impeccable customer attention. Both the internal (employees) customer and the external (end-users) customers are at risk. In addition to seeking your marketshare, they also want your "already trained" personnel with already developed "skill sets."

While all of these factors are critical factors, impeccable customer attention takes precedence over all others since the best products and pricing can be overshawdowed by the "feelings" of people, particularly customers and employees. When people feel good about an organization, they will protect the organization and the relationship of the organization with its questions. When people feel bad about an organization, well, anything can and will happen. This is the stuff competitive strategies are made of. The only real thing that separates competition from your bottom line are the people impacting and building the bottom line; these can only be employees serving and customers buying.

THE NATURE OF COMPETITION

I find the comparison between the wilderness and the marketplace revealing. Over the years, professionals have joked about "its a jungle out here." I do not feel that they are too far from the truth. The struggle, with a few exceptions, is very similar.

In the jungle, animals instinctly understand that at any given time they are either predator or prey. They understand that survival is hunting for prey to eat and surviving the hunt of other predators seeing them as prey at all times. They recognize that at any given moment, they can be some other animal's meal or that they can make some other animal their meal. They are accutely aware of the fact that fatigue, apathy, over-confidence, and presumptions are tools of the competitors. They never forget this reality.

The only real difference between the jungle and the business market place is that as intelligent and rational human beings, sometimes we just do not understand what the animals never forget; that we are either hunting or being hunted at all times. Perhaps it is because our predators are walking and talking just like us. Perhaps it is because they are exquisitely dressed, speak the king's English, and most of the time, they kill without blood. Perhaps it is because when they have fed off of us we are still left standing—it is rarely sudden death. The reality is that the potential to under-estimate our competitors is predominant and this must change if we are to survive in a global economy.

We must remember at all times that there is very little difference between the jungle and the business marketplace when it comes to competition. Let's examine a few areas:

1. Competition always seek the weakest link. They seek prey that is: alone, unaware, vulnerable, pre-occupied, and comfortable. This is true in the wild as well as in the business market place. The major differences are:

   • Instead of taking your last breath, they take your last dollar.

   • Unlike in the wild, they are willing to take a little at a time.

   • In many cases, the weight of death is slow but very sure.

   • They will take members of your team as members of their team.

   • They will set up housing in your nest by making it their nest.

2. In the wild, animals are born with the instincts of survival. In the business environment, the employees at all levels must be taught to fear, to respect, and to ward against competitors as a means of survival. Since this means doing things differently, in many cases employers will meet resistance from the employees. They simply do not believe that there is a fierce battle going on. They must learn about a world of basic survival instincts and the uncom-

promising realities. Unfortunately, many do not learn until it is too late and they find themselves in the unemployment line as a result of layoffs, downsizing, and re-engineering.

3. In the wild, predators operate on the element of speed and surprise. In the business environment our competitors don't need for us to close our eyes—we need only to blink.

4. Competitive excellence is a matter of survival. Survival is a composite of strategic decisive moves. Make the right move at the right time and you earn the right to make another. The struggle is continuous. Success is never final and failure is not always fatal. However, make a single error at the wrong time and death is swift merciless, and inevitable. Sometimes we just have to seek reincarnation.

5. Like the animals in the wild, our people must recognize that at all times, they are both predator and prey. We are always one or the other if we hold anything of value to the marketplace. The game is played out daily whether you see it or not.

6. Like in the wild, employees must recognize that the relationship between predator and prey is fascinating, complex, and ever-evolving. Employees must relish it, prepare for it, and play the game with finesse and finality. The hunt is always going on and they should be ever mindful of the attempts and of the attacks.

7. It should be known that vulnerable fat areas will be hit first—look for the ambush. As in the wild, it should be known that competition is watching you long before they strike. This game called competition is about wit and the survival of the fittest. If you snooze, you lose.

8. Our employees must be alerted, that the competitor is choosy. They want what you want. The only thing standing in their way is you—you are the TARGET.

9. Like in the wild, the drama of survival doesn't always come with a happy ending. Some members must be sacrificed so that others might live. This is evidenced through lay-offs, etc.

10. Competition, be it the death of an animal or the death of a business, is still death and all in a days work . . . only the strong will survive.

DIVERSITY AND COMPETITIVE THREATS

If you agree with my observation on competition, then the Diversity factor should be evident. The improper focus on Diversity in the eyes of competition could be just the opening the competitor is seeking. Diversity improperly positioned could very well mean "Diversion." Any activity that is not working for the mission is working against the mission. Rejecting other team members is a diversion from the undisputed goal of gaining and maintaining market share through customer satisfaction and warding off competitive threats. This diversion signals opportunity to competitors who are always seeking weaknesses in your armour. Please allow me to indulge and share with you how the competitive factor works for and against the Diversity factor.

We have agreed that competition takes no prisoners. We have also agreed that for competitive purposes, *you are the target.* The success of your competitor depends on your failure to protect your customer base by any means necessary.

THE UNDISPUTED TRUTH

Diversity, unfortunately, has become another buzzword to many. Some see it as another cut at Equal Opportunity and Affirmative Action. There is a danger in that because while it is a frequently discussed topic, the ability or inability to recognize, respect, and to reward the management of the diversity equation will determine the fate of organizations worldwide.

It is no secret, minorities and women are entering the workforce at a rate of seven to one compared to the white male. This is nothing to boast about. It is another weakness in our armour. We need everyone from everywhere. We must be able to relate to our customers. Since we do not know who our customers are, we would be wise to include everyone. My response to the odds of white males to minorities and females is: so what, what are they going to do when they get there? Business survival has less to do with numbers of bodies and more to do with numbers of dollars.

Mastering the Diversity equation in the business environment is only important to the degree that it impacts business—and it does! Competition penetrates market share through holes. Opportunities created when "teams" are not really teams. The size of the hole determines the size of the market share lost. Any hole is too large in today's competitive environment. The only true measurement of the effects of competitive penetration is the bottom line—your bottom line.

FACTORS TO CONSIDER

Everything we knew as right and perfect is under seige. The home, the workplace, the church, etc. Things that were are no more. It is as if when we finally found the answers, someone changed all of the questions.

The global competitive environment is multi-dimensional. In addition to competing head-on for users of products and services from an employer standpoint, many Americans feel that they are also competing with foreign countries for jobs. Much of the labor that was being perfomed in America is being transferred out of the U.S. because of cheaper labor.

A further extension of this multi-dimensional feat is that many people from foreign countries have made America their home and are now setting up businesses right here in the U.S. Among other challenges, foreigners come to the U.S. prepared and honored to learn to speak our language as a means of survival. In many cases Americans are sluggish about learning other languages. This sluggishness negates the ability to gain employment in American-based foreign establishments.

An even further extension is the new revelation of a "Global-minded General Electric" making the decision to "go where the growth is." The November 8, 1993 issue of *Business Week* revealed that the company's executives are "betting on the three developing giants—China, India and Mexico, with Southeast Asia close behind." This decision is good for the company but the Union of Electrical Workers argues that U.S. laws should prohibit international growth that takes American jobs overseas. This is just the beginning or the end, depending on how you look at it.

We are in a true world economy and "prospecting for sales" could be "letting your fingers do the walking" to Albany or Amsterdam. The line of boundaries is getting more and more blurred with every new development of technology. Technology is in itself an entirely new challenge as advances are sudden, often, and for the non-astute, paralyzing.

As the baby boomers start to move into their 50's, companies are developing strategies that involve early retirement. People are living longer, while downsizing and mergers are daily corporate strategies.

As we struggle to manage the unmanageable, the need for flattened organizational structures has become non-negotiable. The emergence of Total Quality Management, Self-Directed Work Teams, cross-training, and other strategies are leading the way in company training rooms and executive board rooms. All are designed to enhance customer satisfaction, productivity, employee morale, and profits while warding off competitive intrusion. It is a real jungle out there.

WHAT DOES IT ALL MEAN?

It means that the strategy is in the people and the strategies are always under construction. The only thing that matters is "gray matter." We are deep into an information society and as great minds work to "enhance" the "Information Super Highway," astute leaders are charting pathways to survival on the speedway of success. It is no longer about how people look (if it ever was). It is about how they think. Do they think? How long do they think?

The focus is so much on just pure undiluted "thinking" that some organizations are relegating the task to computers, external consultants, and designated think tanks. How's that for "different?"

The only known factors are: Change, Challenge, Flexibility, and Leadership at all levels.

THAT WAS THEN—THIS IS NOW

One of the greatest challenges facing the experienced worker is "letting go." Letting go of old realities while taking hold of new possibilities. Reminiscing about the old workplace will only serve as a past-time of daydreaming which could lead to a full-time daydreaming predicament. The workplace that promised stability, predictability, job security and a defined job description is gone forever. That was then, this is now.

The old workplace prided itself in long-term hiring and paid vacations that brought in temporaries for relief. Now "permanent is temporary" and "temporary is permanent." Organizations are getting real comfortable with "contracting out." Upward mobility is now just "picking yourself up" in the area of morale as more and more uncertainties threaten the ability to earn a guarantee of permanent employment.

Employees must find a way to manage their own mentality in the midst of uncertainty. They must measure their skill level and be prepared to upgrade that skill level by any means necessary. This is imperative to ensure that they can add value to their respective organizations and avoid the possibility of layoff. While organizations are frantically attempting to provide the development needed, technology is making the task more than challenging. The employee must protect his position by defining luck as: "preparation meeting opportunity." Staying ready to keep from getting ready.

Trust and loyalty are necessary ingredients to productivity. These factors are under seige as organizations struggle to make the necessary "cuts" to "size" the organization. To be effective and to minimize disruption, the element of surprise is needed. When the gavel falls on the designated employee, they feel ambushed. The remaining "witnesses" are now wondering "will I be next?" How much trust and loyalty can we expect?

The answer is: as much as needed to accomplish the task. We are having to learn personal and professional trust and loyalty and to live as the recovering alcoholic: one day at a time. We simply must be "good enough to stay and good enough to go."

While many do not agree which much of what is going on, we must admit that it is a long awaited wake up call. Maximum response to customer demand should not be driven by competitive threats. However, competition is now driving the economy and now the customer is getting the respect that they have always deserved—but at what price?

The price is "total commitment" and a functional partnership between employee and employer. We have finally arrived at the reality that "we are all in this together."

THE TOTALITY OF THE TEAM AND THE GAMES OF WEAK LINK AND POP THE WHIP

Many of us remember a game we played growing up called "WEAK LINK." A circle would be formed with a group of people joining hands with one person in the middle. The only way the person could escape the circle was to break the circle by force. The mission of the circle was to hold on tight to each other to avoid penetration of the circle. Of course, the person inside of the circle would survey the circle looking for weaknesses to "break through." Once s/he saw what looked like a possibility, s/he would attack that area with force. Sometimes it worked, and sometimes what appeared to be weak was, in fact, very strong. The objective was to find a "weak link."

One thing is for sure; if there was a person in the circle who felt that s/he did not belong in the circle or for any reason did not feel enough loyalty to protect the circle, the circle was broken. When it all boiled down, it was how the people making up the circle felt. The same is true for organizations. This is the real purpose of Diversity awareness—to eliminate the possibilities of "weak links." To put it more succinctly to seal in the marketshare and seal out competitors.

"Pop the whip" worked a little differently in that it would be a straight line. Each person acted as an independent entity whose survival depended on holding on and moving with the flow as the direction would change. All in the line would run very fast and "at will" the leader would attempt to change the direction of the group "without warning." This would cause an abrupt about face and disorientation because you had to change direction without notice. You had to think, move, hold on and recover without losing momentum since the line ahead of you would continue to move. If a break was made, you and everyone behind you would be disconnected and eliminated from the competition.

The objective was to keep up with the whip without breaking the chain. While this too, is indicative of workplace growing, it is more a description of what is going on in the world. The organizations are lined up and running at a very fast pace. At will, competition, customers and/or technology can and will change directions without warning and we must keep up without breaking the chain. If we are not successful, we too will be disconnected and eliminated from the competition. Each team is only as strong as the people within that team and the ability to hold on in the midst of sudden changes.

It is the responsibility of the organization to change directions with sudden changes and without losing momentum. This requires a total team effort. The team is only as strong as its weakest link.

THE INTERNAL STRUGGLE MUST END

No game was ever played and won without a total team effort. Each person must have a meaningful role and must feel valued. Each person must understand that the first role is to value the other roles. Unless this happens, then we will simply not be in the game. When the chain is broken, then we instantly move from predator to prey. This must not happen.

Diversity is the ultimate in team building and build teams, we must. We need all of the players and we need players who can make plays without regard for race, gender, sexual orientation, disabilities, etc. The mission is to survive.

A healthy respect for Diversity must be second nature and it must be recognized as a means to an end—it is not an end within itself. It can be compared to learning to drive an automobile, once the lesson is learned, the reactions become automatic. The automobile becomes just that a vehicle to take you to another place and time for a greater mission. The same is true for Diversity. Once we master it, we must move on and let it take us where we want to go. The destination is victory! We must not waste too much time on this. We have invested too much time on it already.

How much time is too much time? A better question is: How much more can we afford the eroding of our economy? How many more lay-offs can we afford? How much more effort can we afford to "redirect" from competitive intrusion and customer satisfaction to focus on the so called "differences" of our internal team members? I challenge you to answer these questions. We will then have the answer to the first question: how much time is too much time?

CHAPTER IV

THE SHAPING OF INTELLECTUAL EXCELLENCE

Walter B. Wriston, former chairman of Citicorp, in his book, "The Twilight of Sovereignty," talks about how the information revolution is transforming our world. . . . He makes an observation worthy of quoting:

Instant information does not in and of itself create understanding. Thinking about the whole explosion of information and the way that it is transmitted throughout the world, one might visualize a pyramid: At the bottom of the pyramid are data; the next layer up is information culled from all of the data; the next layer up is our experience. Each individual is the product to some extent of the velocity of his or her own experience, and it is information filtered through that experience that in the best of circumstances creates wisdom at the top of the pyramid.

The new electronic infrastructure of the world turns the whole planet into a market for ideas, and the idea of freedom has proved again and again that it will win against any competing idea. We are thus witness to a true revolution; power really is moving to the people. pg 176

Walter B. Wriston
Former Chairman, Citicorp

While the entire thought is provocative, what is sobering is the observation that he makes about filtering information through experience. He observes that when information is filtered through personal experience, in the best of circumstances this creates wisdom at the top of the pyramid. I will say that pyramid is the organization or corporation.

If one were to create an equation, it would read: information plus experience = wisdom. To look mathematical: $I + E = W$. Somewhere in the good book it says, wisdom is the principal thing; therefore get wisdom: and with all thy getting get understanding. From the Business Book to the Bible Book, the message is the same—get wisdom and get understanding.

Another point made by Mr. Wriston is:

When information technology made information the most important factor of production, it made the timely acquisition of the best information the number-one-goal of business management. pg 111 The job of instilling such goals has much to do with persuasion, teaching, and leadership than with old-style management. Successful business leaders are finding that the skills of a good political leader are more relevant than those of the general. pg 117

As information becomes the most important factor of production, good workers and managers must acquire more of it. Former subalterns become formidable experts with specialized skills that may outstrip those of the boss. These people reject autocracy because their talents cannot be efficiently used under the "command and control" model. pg 117 The work required of today's workers depends too much on creativity, autonomy, and personal judgment to be successfully regimented. pg 119

Workers who work by thinking cannot be as easily monitored. They must be motivated, well taught, and engaged. pg 120

Today more than ever, having a business strategy means having an information strategy, a strategy for recognizing opportunities in the on rush of change, a strategy for transforming data flows that now look like a necessary evil, into new products, services and sources of profit, a strategy for ensuring that a company derives full value from the knowledge accumulated by its workers rather than allowing that knowledge to languish or leak away. pg 122

Having made these observations about the role of the people in the information age, the next obvious question is: How does this affect the diversity equation? If $I + E = W$, what does it mean when "E" is disregarded, diminished, or disrespected? You got it! "I" and "W" walks right out of the door seeking and new factor: "R" for respect.

What is needed more than ever is not just intellect but intellectual excellence. It is not good enough to be literate, smart, or even competent. The key is to "out-think" your competitors. Out-thinking competitors means unbridled access to information. It means feeling good about ourselves. It means a total team that knows that it is a total team—the operative word is "total."

Shaping intellectual excellence means freeing the mind from unnecessary distractions. It means freeing people to know that we are here to win "whatever it takes." It means letting people know that *RISK* is needed; and therein lies the problem.

RISK is risky. Webster defines risk as follows: "The possibility of meeting danger or suffering harm or loss, exposure to this." The "R" in risk means responsible and accountable—for your actions. Unfortunately, to many people this responsibility and accountability was freely given but it did not come with the proper level of authority to get things done or unconditional forgiveness when something went wrong.

For many, this is a risk that is too great to take. This is particularly true in an unhealthy environment as it relates to the Diversity equation. It is very difficult to conceive of taking a risk in an environment where your very presence and your right to exist is challenged.

To better understand the impact of this, particularly as it relates to the Diversity equation, let's use a popular scenario—Maslow's Hierarchy of Needs. Maslow's Hierarchy was developed by a psychologist named Dr. Abraham Maslow who determined that people functioned basically out of five different needs at all times. These needs are influencing our behavior at all times. The needs are described as a hierarchy because, according to Dr. Maslow, until the need on one level is satisfied, the individual will think of nothing else.

To indulge you in an example: Let's examine the physiological need. Let's assume that you have been stranded on a desert for two days without water. If someone came along and offered you two ounces of water or two million dollars, you would without question and without hesitation, take the water. The reason is simple, you can not live without water. Your mission is to first, survive. Until the physiological need is satisfied, no other need matters. The hierarchy progresses upward as each need is achieved. A review of these needs follows.

Dr. Maslow described those needs as: (1) physiological—this need deals with those things needed to survive, i.e. water, food, etc. as demonstrated in the above example. (2) security or safety—the need to preserve the quality of life, i.e. insurance, guarantees, etc. (3) social—the need for acceptance (4) esteem—this particular need has a caveat in that there are two areas of esteem: a) self esteem and b) the esteem of others. Dr. Maslow says that before one can gain the esteem of others, one must first have self esteem. It is in the esteem area of need that competence and competition reside where people will RISK it all to achieve recognizing that RISK means doing things that have never been done before. The final need is (5) self actualization.

It is felt by Dr. Maslow that the first four needs are deficit needs in that the role of others and the approval of others is critical in the achievement of these needs. Self actualization is a competition with yourself. You are not seeking anyone's approval but your own. It is when you come face-to-face with your mortality. It is the area where one is consumed with making a difference in pursuit of a personal legacy.

For our purposes, let's focus on need number four, esteem. Ideally, this is the level of production for teams on the move. People who function at this level are self assured, competent (knowing what you know and knowing what you do not know). These people are striving to discover what they do not know without fear of ridicule or repercussion. They are taking risks and making discoveries. They are making discoveries about their work, the organization, themselves, and everything around them. They are truly shaping their own intellectual excellence. They are living up to the mission in the workplace. The mission in the workplace is to shape intellectual excellence. My definition of excellence is simple: it is your unconditional best. In the best of all worlds, this describes the ideal employee.

When the Diversity equation enters the picture, in many cases it is not the best of all worlds, in fact, it could be hell. If an individual's body could be considered as hardware and the mind of the individual is considered software, we would have a worthy comparison; one that is appropriate for the "information age."

Imagine having a computer and someone told you to be careful with it because computers from that manufacturer have been known to malfunction. You would immediately begin to seek ways to protect yourself. First, you would ensure that you had back-up copies of all of the software you installed in the computer. Secondly, you would ensure that you backed up everything that you input into the computer—just in case something happened.

The bottom line is that you just do not have confidence in that computer. All of your involvements with that computer would be a series of suspicion, backing up, and hesitancy. You would not operate with a clear head and if that computer could "feel" it would eventually start to live up to this self-fulfilling prophecy. Your intellectual excellence would be severely altered because instead of concentrating on your work, you are concentrating on "not losing data or time." The likelihood of that computer changing is slim and none. Like the human being, what you get is what you get.

Chances are if someone came in and offered you another computer by that manufacture, you would refuse. Never mind that though you were told of the unreliability of this unit, you have never experienced any of it. In fact, now that you think of it, it has been one of the best computers you have ever used. But you rationalize that your colleague knew what he was talking about. And surely you were just lucky with this unit. You are not going to push your luck by taking on another one.

It is a great thing that we are talking about a computer. A person on the other had would be different. Because they do have feelings and unfortunately, they tend to respond to your expectations. They would observe the hesitancy and the backing up and the distrust of his or her performance. Chances are, you would experience a self-fulfilling prophecy. Not because it was true, but because people have feelings and they have needs. They are driven by the needs at all times.

Many times there are several people experiencing this dilemma as in Maslow's Hierarchy, perhaps they did not make it past the social needs. On one hand they are accepted by those like themselves but rejected by those unlike themselves.

As they sit down to have coffee with those in the "same boat" they talk about all of their observations and ideas but also acknowledge that to implement those ideas would mean taking a risk. Since there is a general distrust of their "kind" and a general lack of trust of their work, a mistake *could* cost them their job. So as a result, they do only what is *safe*.

This really happens. A case in point is the October 31, 1993 show of "60 Minutes," the U.S. Marines were being accused of racism. A high ranking General went on National television with the declaration that African Americans in general, could not swim, shoot, or read a compass in the dark as well as others. While he later came back and retracted his statement after receiving pressure, the thought process is still there. That was 1993! The generalization was absurd. However, because of his rank, many well meaning and unsuspecting leaders under his influence would adopt his stereotypical observations as fact and many African-Americans would suffer, especially the U.S. Marines.

How many excellent marksmen, swimmers, and masters of direction have been erroneously denied an opportunity to shine because of such careless generalizations?

Many professionals with the real talent needed to succeed, interacting with such irresponsible leaders would soon fall short of their own potential. Because of preconceived notions coupled with position and authority, they will spend countless hours proving something that should never be discussed and will be preoccupied with self preservation of pride instead of performance.

They will never make it to level four in the esteem category of the hierarchy because before one can gain the esteem of others, one must first have self esteem. They feel pretty good about themselves, however, they recognize that others have predetermined and unsubstantiated ideas about their capabilities— so they just play it safe. In many cases they defy the odds and take the risks only to be destroyed.

They never reach level four for fear of being relegated back to level one. This individual's intellectual excellence will never be achieved in that environment. They are in intellectual bondage and until they are freed, the company will be in intellectual bondage. This bondage must be broken before intellectual excellence can be achieved.

If we are to shape the intellectual excellence in the workplace, we must first agree that each individual in the workplace is worthy of being there. We must be prepared to reward those who recognize and relish this fact. We must be prepared to reprimand anyone who does not recognize and relish this fact. People repeat what is rewarded and we must inspect what we expect.

I am reminded of a fictitious story during the initial stages of integration. A group of Negroes (as called before the Black and African American era) people went into a restaurant to eat. As they sat down in the booth, the waitress came over and immediately said to them: "we don't serve colored folks in here!" One of the men looked up and replied, "that's good ma'am 'cause all we want is chicken."

We must take the moral of that story to the 90's and beyond. As people start to express their preferences about what they like and do not like about people, we must declare that "all we want is thinking." We want people who are prepared to think, learn, do, and teach.

In my mind, Diversity has nothing to do with people and everything to do with winning through people. I do not see Diversity as an end. I see it as a means to an end. I see it as a common sense approach to winning. Liking or disliking people has no place in the workplace. This kind of thinking, in my mind, is unproductive and unprofessional. We must adapt a sports mentality and play to win. We can not win until we recognize talent without regard for race, gender, physical challenge, etc.

What we must train ourselves to do is to look at the overall goal and then find the components to satisfy that goal. We should be looking at experience, training, talent, temperment, style—all of these things are gender and race neutral. Sometimes, you might need to focus on gender, race, or some other "unique characteristic" in the accomplishment of a worthy goal. We should have resolved our issues in the workplace so that when and if this becomes necessary as a strategy, it is also understood as a competitive tactic.

I can recall as a field sales representative during the 1970's in a very strategic account, I called on on a man that was obviously uncomfortable with me. I recognized that he was not accustomed to seeing a woman or a minority in this capacity and probably was confused at facing both at once.

Without acknowledging my observations, I immediately dismissed myself and reserved the right to return at a later date. I engaged one of my white colleagues to accompany me on the return call the following week while openly explaining my suspicions and my empathy for the customer. I introduced her as my regional manager so he would not expect to see her again. My mission was to sell him a copier not a color.

I had no problems with his discomfort, in fact, I found the empathy to understand it. Because I felt good about myself, I could suspend my anxieties in order to respond to his needs, I was able to gain a very strategic account. Perhaps he saw through my little caper, perhaps he did not. However, because I was able to override my anxieties, it paved the way for what was to become a very fruitful relationship. I did not judge him. I felt that it was my responsibility to find common ground between us. I needed to get out of my own way to help him to get over his discomfort—and he did. We both grew as a result.

Everyone must acknowledge and accept that intellectual excellence is not the main thing—it is the only thing. We must clearly understand that in many ways, we are hardware and software. To that end, we must work at recognizing the fact that at any time and at will, a person can choose to take his/

her hardware out of our environment and with their hardware goes their software with our company secrets housed within. Unfortunately, we cannot erase the programming as in the computer; and try as we might once they leave we are not protected. If a mind is a terrible thing to waste, it is a more terrible thing to develop and then lose to competitors.

If we are to shape intellectual excellence, people must be free to be themselves. The greatest expression is personal self expression. We must free people to listen to the beat of their own drum within our band. They must be at peace to sense their own intuitive approach to competitive threats and customer satisfaction. They must be cherished and inspired so that they feel the commitment needed to be self propelled when it comes to learning and teaching. At all cost, we must ensure that their morale is enhanced and monitored at all times. We must engage them in our realities and we must engage in their realities. The mutuality of employer and employee is a predominant factor, finally.

If we are to really be effective and successful, we must learn that for each "difference" there is another approach to "thinking." As an organization, that is one more base we can cover. When we can send the message that what we want is universal appeal and to appeal universally, we must be universal, then we will have arrived as a city, nation, as a world, and mostly as an organization.

We should see "internal differences" as "internal demographics." This enables us to respond to all of the external demographics and to better understand and serve our customer base. We must remember that we pull customers, employees and competitors from the same base. To the degree that we are balanced in our internal demographics, we can employ a balanced strategy to gain and to maintain customers. More importantly, it levels the playing field when warding off competitive threats if we can understand what they are "thinking."

Once we gain the profile of our target, then we know who to consult within our organization that could have the inside track.

We must stop the paranoia, self doubt, backing-up, and all of the other self defeating activities associated with broad generalities based on physical and cultural differences. We must stop the hysteria about the "differences."

We have too much real work to do—we can no longer afford the luxury of infighting. It is true, "a mind is a terrible thing to waste"— we don't have a mind to waste. The only thing worse than losing a trained mind is confusing a trained mind and keeping it in your work environment. We must decide for once and for all "if a person is here, they belong here." Our job is to ensure that they know what the overall goal is and what their role is in achieving that overall goal. Nothing else matters.

Shaping intellectual excellence is about freeing people to be dynamically themselves. It is about having a sense of purpose, a sense of belonging. We must view Diversity and every other strategy as a strategy to preserve the competitive edge, to gain and maintain market share, and to create a universal think tank to ensure a balanced approach to the market place. It must be a part of the strategy to win.

When people feel good about who they are, they also feel good about everything and everyone they come into contact with. A happy person makes an ecstatic employee. Ecstatic employees produce ecstatic customers. Ecstatic customers "reduce" competitive threats and that is the bottom line.

CHAPTER V

THE TOTALITY OF EXCELLENCE EQUALS THE SUM OF THE PARTS

This is a make or break decade. Humanity's future is in the balance.

Ed Wilson
The Diversity of Life

Ed Wilson in his book *The Diversity of Life* expresses concern over the extinction of plants, insects, and animals. He says:

If we let too many species go, we face an enormous psychological and spiritual loss.

While Mr. Wilson is talking about the wilderness, he could very well be talking about the workplace. How many times have we heard the predictions for the year 2000. In all of the figures being shared by experts, the predominant reality is that about three out of every four employees entering the workforce will be minorities and women. Of course, you have heard the observation about the diminishing white male. I do not feel that the onslaught of one race and gender in the face of the diminishing numbers of another is the answer. We need all sexes and races to win this war and this includes the white male. Are we any different from the wild? I don't think so. It is clear to me that the same observations Mr. Wilson is making about the wilderness is true about the workplace—there is no need to adjust the language.

We can no more be successful in a workplace without white males than we can be in a workplace without Diversity. We are all components of the totality of the whole and we each have our respective role. In my mind, if there is a role that is critical in what we have to do, it is the white male. He has the most critical role of all in that he was first in the workplace. He wrote all of the rules—adjustments are now needed. The adjustments need to reflect a heterogeneous workplace instead of one dominated by white males.

The adjustments need to reflect the presence of the people with disabilities, the different sexual orientations, the different cultures, and all of the other unique factors that were not known or acknowledged factors in the beginning. While, in many cases, reinvention is needed, we must not attempt to re-write the rules in totality, we must collaborate to determine what needs to be thrown out, what needs to be kept in place, and what simply needs a little tweaking.

The white male is not going to sit idle and accept exclusion any more than women and minorities did. We do not have time for another battle, we have a war to win. A war against poverty, technology, and the sheer quality of life. We need not focus negatively on the differences any longer.

We must seek universal appeal from all sides and while we must admit that the white males are the authors of the plan, we must also acknowledge that others, under different circumstances would have contributed if given the opportunity. That opportunity is presenting itself now. We can argue the point of who is right and who is wrong, however, the reality is that if there is a right, it is simply "dead right." A person maintaining the "right of way" in the face of ongoing traffic will be just as dead as if he had been wrong. We can not unscramble eggs. We can only decide what to do with them before we lose the opportunity. When it comes to the state of the workplace, we cannot unscramble the eggs but together, we can make a powerfully good omelette.

Mr. Wilson, as he observes the "marvelous diversity" of our planet declares:

> *. . . all living species are survivors, shaped and honed by billions of acts of natural selection. All are very good at something. . . .*

Our mission is to create the environment where everyone feels free to find out what they are good at and to make that contribution to the total effort of the organization.

Because the bottom line is the only line that matters in measuring tangible success, we must not limit ourselves to how we construct that line. We must recognize that on the otherside of that line are customers and competitors. Our mission is to match the diversity of our clientele and the profile of our competitors. We must speak all languages, fade into any environment, we must neutralize all genders and celebrate all differences. We can best do that through having a Diverse workforce that understands and demonstrates "universal appeal."

> *"Loss of diversity has an insidious consequence. In the event of global climate change, diversity will help determine which ecosystems collapse and which flourish."*

As I write this book, AT&T is under siege because of the insensitivity of a publication. Marching in front of its headquarters are minority protesters demanding appropriate action and declaring that if the representation of minority employees at higher levels was built into the company, a publication of this nature would not have been created. Maybe they are right, maybe they are wrong. However, once again, are we looking at "dead right?"

How much time, money, and productivity is being lost because of this. What is happening to the image of AT&T? If the minority factor was not there, would they be under siege? Is anything totally right or totally wrong? What is happening to the productivity of those minorities who feel that they have been treated fairly by AT&T? Why are we still, after 30 years, having this conversation? I do not know the answer to these questions. I can only speculate. However, I will submit that there is more collapsing going on than flourishing. Perhaps not enough to shut them down but enough to gain the attention of every vehicle and pedestrian on Peachtree Street, along with newspaper, television, and radio coverage. Negative coverage. The parts are fragmented and so is productivity.

I would submit that conversations are going on between employees within AT&T and in some cases, anxiety and hostility is being experienced. Morale is being eroded and productivity is being lost. There is no totality of effectiveness because the sum total of the parts are divided.

Will this issue be resolved in our lifetime? If we are fighting the same fight after 30 years, what will happen to those coming behind us? Have we left a legacy of leadership or a let down? We must fix it for us, we must fix it for our offsprings. It is a senseless battle. It is a losing battle. We simply must pick up the mantle of leadership and deal with the reality of what is facing us that can be changed and that which is changing in spite of our efforts to maintain the status quo.

No one is totally right or totally wrong. However, if we do not find a way to reason together. We will all be "dead right."

Signals abound that the lost of life's diversity endangers not just the body but the spirit. If that much is true, the changes occurring now will visit harm on all generations to come.

Ed Wilson
The Diversity of Life
U.S. News and World Report *pg. 61–67*

On another note, let's look at America's favorite past-time, Baseball. The team has nine people. A pitcher, a first, second, and third baseman, a shortstop, left fielder, center fielder, and right fielder. The pitcher and the catcher form the battery.

The game starts at the pitchers mound and although the pitcher determines when the game starts, s/he is usually a weak hitter and when it is time to bat, he usually bats ninth. *That is not right or wrong, it just is.* The object of the game is to win. The manager lists the batting order before each game and players must bat in that order throughout the game. You can bet that s/he develops the list to win without regard for anything other than skill.

The lead-off man or the first batter should be fast and a good hitter. The second batter should be able to advance the lead-off batter. The third, fourth, and fifth batters are considered "clean up" hitters and are expected to hit the ball with distance to bring in the previous batters. The sixth hitter is able to get on base fairly often and the seventh and eighth hitters are expected to bring him in. Again, the pitcher is usually the ninth hitter. A batter has less than half a second to decide whether he will swing at a ball. The choice is his or hers, the consequence is the team's.

The totality of effectiveness truly equals the sum total of the parts. There are nine people. Each chosen for their unique contribution to the team. In the case where the possibility of falling short occurs, there are pinch hitters and relief pitchers. The object of the game is to win. If you had all pitchers, winning would not be possible because pitchers are not great hitters. If you had all hitters, winning would not be possible because their skill is in hitting not pitching. There is one game to play and at the end it will be won or lost. The manager must determine the components of a "winning game" and identify those components in different players without regard for anything other than the ability to contribute that component in such a way that victory is eminent.

If you took away even one player, or one talent, you would then take away one ninth of the players and probably 100 percent of the ability to win. With the exception of roving responsibilities, baseball challenges are no different then challenges in the workplace. We need players who can make plays.

While we in the workplace come in different packages, those packages house talent. We have a responsibility as a manager or leader, to unwrap the package to reveal the talent with unconditional positive expectations. As a package, we have the responsibility to present ourselves as a package housing talent that can help to win. We must not let our past experiences, anxieties, or preconceived notions about those who are different send the signal that we are a ticking bomb waiting to explode into a class action suit. We must all learn to trust again.

As we progress deeper in the 90's, we are moving further and further from the baseball example. While the decisions about who will come up to bat and when, will in many cases be proactive, it could change. Also, we will not always have the benefit of a manager to make this determination. As we move into an era of self directed work teams, the manager could be any leader who has proven him or herself worthy.

We will not always have the luxury of first, second, third, etc. in the pursuit of success. The one up to bat, in many cases will be the one nearest the mound when the "pitcher/competitor" decides to pitch. Assignments are getting to be more and more interchangeable and cross-training is becoming an offensive strategy rather than an option.

One thing is for certain, the name of the game is still winning. There will be a winner and a loser in every contest. The winning team will be the team where every player understands where the goal is and what is necessary to reach that goal. Every player will understand that there is one team, one game, many players, and one verdict. They will understand that the totality of effectiveness equals nothing more than the sum of the parts. We each have one vote. It should be a vote of confidence in our peers and colleagues. We need teamwork, self motivation, and unconditional commitment.

If there is only one half second to decide, there is no time to doubt. No time to doubt your worth or the worth of any team member.

Universal appeal is a critical factor and each person must seek translucence with the focus on winning and enhancing the overall team. The times are paradoxical in that on one hand we must seek teamwork, on the other hand, we must seek out "career best." We must strive as individuals to be the best that we have ever been. We must remember the old adage that "a high tide lifts all ships."

QUESTIONS ABOUT THIS CHAPTER

1. What is your initial reaction to the foregoing?

2. Does it compare to what you have experienced?

3. What have you observed in the workplace that would contradict or confirm the foregoing?

4. What would you add to the chapter you have just read?

5. What do you see as potential solutions?

Recommendation: Choose a person or a group of persons of different gender, culture, race, etc. and initiate a discussion with the intent being:

1. Enlightenment.

2. Developing a functional action plan personally.

3. Exploring the possibilities of developing a functional action plan for the immediate work area.

CHAPTER VI

THE ULTIMATE AND THE ONLY MISSION:

Unconditional Sharing of Information To Maintain The Competitive Edge

Of all of the goals and proposed missions one might conjure up, none is more important than the unconditional transfer of information among members of a designated team. I am convinced that there are no "defined" solutions, only "potential solutions." The solutions needed by organizations are housed in the hearts and the minds of the people. The skillful, uninhibited and complete release of the flow of information is the only real hope for the surviving and thriving of organizations worldwide. The continuous tug of war in the Diversity equation threatens the ability to do this.

APPOINTED DUTY AND THE KISS OF DEATH

The reason the issue of Diversity is an issue is because there are people in the work place who do not believe that others should be there because of sex, race, and other differences. They consider it their "appointed duty" to do something about it. The mission of these people is to drive the people with "differences" out of the organization or at least to suppress their accomplishments. The mission of the people of the perceived "differences" is to survive. Both are withholding information to the detriment of the organization in support of their own personal agendas. The internal battle goes on at the expense of productivity. As long as we are preoccupied with the unresolved issue of Diversity, we are in fact diverted away from the uninhibited and complete release of the flow of information. This is the kiss of death for organizations with any intent to survive the 90's and beyond.

CORNERSTONE OF SURVIVAL

Effective information and the application of this information in pursuit of solutions is the cornerstone of survival. We must understand our companies, our customers, and last but not least, our competitors. Overlay that with the ever changing rate of technology and we do not have time or the luxury of downplaying anyone with a brain inside of our organization. It must be noted that people who do not respect the "differences" within the organization can not possibly respect the differences outside of the organization. This is a walking mine waiting to explode since our customers as well as our competitors will present these same "differences."

Our effectiveness depends on our ability to extract information from everyone without regard for our personal "idiosyncrasies."

When we can not override our own idiosyncrasies, we create anxiety in others. Buying, selling, and thinking is hard enough without having to protect your right to exist.

In her book, *Danger in the Comfort Zone,* Judith M. Bardwick states:

> *When anxiety is very high, people want the sense that they are protected from idiosyncratic behavior or prejudiced attitudes on the part of those who control what happens to them. They want the protection of fairness built into the system. p.106*

When we visit the Diversity equation, it reeks of idiosyncratic behaviors and prejudiced attitudes. This breeds anxiety and anxiety breeds fear. If we go back to Maslow's Hierarchy we know that this propels the individual to need level number two (security/safety). As we discussed, when one need is not satisfied, the individual will not focus on anything else.

Judith Bardwick states that:

> *Fear, anxiety, uncertainty mean the same thing: deep-down panic that your job is in jeopardy and the situation is out of your control.*

To paraphrase, she states that: Organizations must first:

1. Reduce anxiety by creating mechanisms by which people can earn reasonable levels of security.

2. State the parameters of what can be earned.

3. State the nature of the contract.

4. Spell out the mutual expectations and requirements.

People need to know what is being required and what they can expect.

While Ms. Bardwick's comments are made regarding the layoff environment, the same is true for any environment threatening one's security.

AND THE WINNER IS . . . COMPETITION

It must be acknowledged that those who are in resentment of the Diversity equation are not ignorant to the insecurity and anxiety caused by excluding or ridiculing those perceived to be unworthy of being a team member. The creation of insecurity is a tactic of the perpetrator in the overall strategy to drive them out of the workplace. They honestly believe that they are right and that they and everyone on the team will be better off if this person or persons were not there. While the strategy of the perpetrator makes sense to him/her, they must recognize that the person perceived to be unworthy has a strategy of his/ her own. Withholding or distorting information is the favorite strategy of both. And the winner is: C O M P E T I T I O N.

A TIME OF INTERIM SOLUTIONS

The message must be sent loud and clear; there is only one mission: Unconditionally sharing information to maintain the competitive edge. We must inspect what we expect. We must build the spirit of this mission into performance appraisals. We must walk our talk. Everyone must be made aware of the fact that, there are no "complete" thoughts or solutions. We are living in a time of "interim solutions." Interim until technology or competition declares it obsolete. The value of the individual will be as great as his or her last thought and the ability of that individual to come up with ideas and innovations. The worth of the individual will continue to be evolutionary because that is how the human brain works. What is working today is human intelligence.

PURITY OF THOUGHT

All over the place people are recognizing that they can make a UNIQUE contribution. They are recognizing that tenure, age, race sex, and all other defining characteristics are just that, defining characteristics that make them special as a human being to be treasured. These defining characteristics have their place but not in the workplace, unless it is to better understand the workers to better serve the customer and to ward off competition—that's it. Everyone must be thinking and rethinking at all times. We need *purity of thought*. The contamination of the thought process by ridiculous assertions of bigotry must be snuffed out like a bad disease. It *is* a bad disease and it is deadly!

We must learn to see every mind as a potential solution and the back-board to our own thought process. People in the workplace must act as two dull knives. Alone they are just a dull knife—when the cutting edges are rubbed against each other each knife becomes sharp. So it is in the workplace. We must come together in one big electrifying arena to stop the deterioration of opportunity.

Yes, there must be a re-definition of the workplace—technology makes it so. However, the only reason that we are laying off instead of re-allocating and re-assigning is because we have not figured out a way to stretch sales into the workplace. Instead, we are shrinking the workplace to meet the sales. That is a ludicrous trend and it must stop. There is a way and all minds must focus on that. If we do not find a way to plug up this slow leak, the pain will continue—we don't have time for the pain.

Information is what we want and information is what we need. It is the beginning of defining of applications. It is the innovation of applications that create solutions to customer needs. Customers buy need satisfaction and that leads to the bottom line—nothing else. Nothing, absolutely nothing, should inter-rupt this process. Nothing will interrupt this process without fatal consequences to the organization.

Every thought is a piece of the human spirit that can never be recaptured. We must capture it the first time. We must share it at all levels. We must recognize that an organization is noth-ing more than the sum total of all of the thoughts that flow within it. We must ensure that this message is understood, respected, and perpetuated. We must seek new and different ways to approach the "think tank." We must continue to strive for purity of thought so that each employee at every level feels compelled to make his or her contribution to the think tank.

We know that people will repeat what is rewarded. We must be poised to recognize and to reward. We must also be prepared to reprimand. People must understand that actions are noth-ing more than the manifestation of thoughts. When it comes to the workplace, we want purity of thought.

TOO BUSY THINKING ABOUT THE BUSINESS AND I *AIN'T* GOT TIME FOR NOTHING ELSE

There was a song years ago by the Temptations and the lyrics were as follows:

I ain't got time to think about money or what it can buy, I ain't got time to discuss the weather or what makes bird-ies fly, and I ain't got time to think about what makes the flowers grow and I never gave it a second thought where the rivers flow . . . too busy thinking about my baby and I ain't got time for nothing else.

While the artist was clearly talking about the love of his life, we must be as serious about what we think in the workplace. Any thought that does not include more ways to win at all levels and in all arenas, is not a pure thought. We must send the message, we must sing the song, we must walk the talk.

When a co-worker approaches with rhetoric and doom and gloom, we must send the message that the response is: "too busy thinking about the business and I ain't got time for nothing else!"

CHAPTER VII

VOLUNTEERISM:

A Leadership Training Ground

As we discuss the need for universal appeal, we are obviously proposing what could appear to be an impossibility. You are probably asking yourself several sensible questions. What happens to the person who is already set in his or her ways with "no time" to go back to school to learn these things? What happens when you decide to take on this new skill and no one else is ready? Isn't there someway to "test the waters" without committing yourself?

I am so glad that you asked these questions. I can answer in one word: Volunteerism. It is by far the best and the most functional training ground of the 90's. Hands-on consequential assignments are always available for self development and results. The greatest reward is that "Excellence Is Transferable." Everything you learn can be transferred to the workplace.

The decade of the 90's has issued a new mandate—one that calls for individual self expression, teamwork, personal accountability and leadership. Many in our society are aggressively searching for new insights into themselves. Most are searching into the skill of leadership.

We have all determined without a doubt that leadership is the single most important ingredient needed to maximize professional and personal opportunities. As we enter the 21st Century, this will be an even greater need.

Many sources are available to gain knowledge about leadership and the common factors contributing to leadership development. Most experts agree: the true leader is defined by those they are attempting to lead. The authentic leader sees him or herself as a servant of the people.

They recognize that the decision to follow the leader, is a discretionary decision. The leader emerges because of the people. The personal power of the leader paves the way for leadership responsibility.

The leader is expected to break new ground. The leader is expected to take the path less traveled. The leader is expected to bring a new dimension to the project or organization. Whereas many are called to serve; *few* are chosen to lead. Leadership development is an ongoing process and a constant race with change. Changes in people, challenges, and the leader him or herself.

It would behoove any leader to not forget this. Hopefully, the leader of the 20th and the 21st Centuries will recognize this in an *humble* and *responsible* way.

He or she recognizes that the honor to lead must be earned everyday in every way; and while there are numerous definitions for leadership and or the word *leader,* none of those words imply coercion or force. Yes, some people are successful in the use of force and coercion for a short time. It is seldom a long-term position and if it is, it is laden with tension.

The leader is usually someone displaying magnetic qualities whereby people are naturally attracted and offer an official or unofficial endorsement of this person as leader.

This endorsement rarely comes as a result of any single definable characteristic. There is usually just this certain something that when present, people feel a certain trust, a certain confidence, a certain motivation. They feel a sense of hope and expectation. They feel that when this person is present—things happen. People feel good about themselves as they prepare to join forces with the leader in the mutual pursuit of some worthy goal.

This person has a reputation. People know who they are, people know their capabilities, people have seen this person in action many, many times.

So does this person have a public relations firm behind him?

Do they have a marketing campaign designed to ensure that the "word" gets out about them and about what they can achieve? The answer is no. What this person has figured out is "the world's best kept secret." This person is a volunteer.

This person has figured out that success in life rarely hinges on what you know or who you know, it hinges on who knows you and who knows what you know.

They have also figured out that to be known is just the beginning, to be known by your work is the ultimate pursuit. They have figured out that serving yourself is easy—to serve others while serving yourself is not only gratifying but developmental.

They have figured out that to develop as a leader, you simply must serve in an unconditional environment with other leaders—it is what strengthens the leadership muscle.

Like the tension needed in body-building to develop the muscles of the body, tension is needed in building the leader. This constructive tension is present in volunteer capacities. Volunteerism is probably the greatest training ground for the person seeking universal appeal.

Working as a volunteer does not eliminate the normal tensions associated with Diversity in the workplace. What it does is to give the individual a new functional arena of less consequence than the workplace.

It gives the individual the opportunity to come face to face with him or herself in a new environment. This helps to give a fresh perspective. It provides a forum for development, if you want it, without repercussion when mistakes are made. In many cases it can provide validation of a discovery made at work.

The lessons learned as a volunteer are transferable because volunteerism is big business. Many people work as hard, if not harder on volunteer responsibilities.

It is a little known fact that the effectiveness and the world economy is built around volunteerism; and not for financial reasons only. In many cases finance is a factor, however this is not the driving force of the volunteer.

Volunteerism brings a factor that money cannot buy. The volunteer brings a combination of value, commitment, and dedication that far exceeds the power of the dollar.

Because of this generic focus and the unconditional commitment, people who experienced tension in working with people of diverse backgrounds in the workplace, find that the same tension does not exist on volunteer projects. A comfort is developed on volunteer projects and this new found comfort is then transferred to the workplace. It is an excellent demonstration of the fact that excellence is transferable.

The leader recognizes this and seeks volunteer opportunities to make his or her contribution to society while at the same time, developing his or her leadership skills.

Meaningful contributions are made because important outcomes are at stake. There are many areas in our society where there is a core team of professionals in place as a catalyst but the real power comes through quality volunteers.

We cannot measure or replace human caring—this is the unique gift of the volunteer. It is this gift of human caring that transcends bigotry, hate, and preconceived ideas into meaningful growth experiences.

Volunteerism goes beyond duty, obligation and responsibility. It is about service, it is about self-gratification, it is about self-denial, and mostly, it is about self-development.

What appears to be incongruent to the average person is evident and obvious to the volunteer, the leader. It is this evidence that makes this self propelled person with the mentality of an Eagle. They understand the tension of "give and take" and the internal "tug of war." They understand that it is this tension that creates and develops the "leader."

The pride and dedication displayed by the volunteer is an accurate emulation of the Eagle—America could never pay for this level of commitment and even if we could, it would soil the power of personal pride. We need more of it in the workplace in general.

America uses the Eagle as a symbol of leadership—it is the symbol of power. No other name so describes the volunteer like the "Eagle." It is personal and professional power at its best. The will and the spirit of the Eagle is indescribable and like the volunteer, the Eagle towers in the face of challenge and adversity.

It is the "stuff" that makes it an Eagle. Always looking for a greater challenge. Always seeing "adversity" as "admonishing". Seeing the *constructive* tension that makes the great even greater. Isn't this what we need in the workplace?

The image of the Eagle, the leader, and the volunteer, is an image to be emulated as major challenges evolve, for that is when the real power of the Eagle, the volunteer and the leader is seen.

The challenges that are always present demand response from those seeing challenges as "food for thought", "tests for development", and "exercise for the leadership muscle."

Storm clouds are often raging in the lives of the leader, the eagle, and the volunteer; but storm clouds bring out the Eagle. They are seldom deterred—only strengthened. Like the Eagle, the leader, the volunteer is unflappable and seamless in their commitment. The eagle and the volunteer understand personal commitment and accountability. They are prepared to pay the price for excellence. They are always serving a greater cause than self.

As we continue to move toward a global society, we will all be tested and tested, and tested. Every opportunity should be taken to get a "leadership workout" when it is available. It is always available as a volunteer. The Diversity, the decisions, and the dedication makes volunteerism a prime leadership training ground.

The way will not always be easy. All worthwhile events will carry challenges—but joining forces with other leaders, utilizing all resources, and activating the dogged determination that only a leader will possess; the volunteer will always come through. There is absolutely no difference in the workplace. Tenacity is needed there more than ever.

So what is it that makes the volunteer leader so reliable, so dedicated, so tenacious? Why is it that more and more citizens of all descriptions are joining forces with the volunteer team? Exactly what is the profile of the volunteer?

THE PROFILE OF THE VOLUNTEER

The profile of the volunteer leader is elusive, expansive and enlightening. However, we can use the acronym of volunteer to shed some light on my perspective.

V **Value added involvement.** Working as a volunteer is usually by choice rather than chance which means that the volunteer brings personal expectation and the potential for personal gratification while making a worthwhile contribution through involvement.

O **Opportunities for growth.** The very nature of volunteerism dictates new and challenging endeavors. Adopting yourself to meet these challenges is a growth process that strengthens.

L **Leadership development.** It is common knowledge that each profession has a recognizable tool. A tool on which the professional relies to test his or her proficiency. For the leader, that tool is leadership ability.

The tool of leadership ability in the leader is difficult to develop. The only way to become proficient is to work with other leaders and other projects that provide validation of your skills, experience and growth.

U **Understanding self and others.** The key to success in any endeavor is knowing yourself and knowing others. It is only through knowing yourself, your strengths, and your weaknesses that you can acknowledge and accept the truth about you.

Then and only then can you amass the power to adapt and allow others to thrive without feeling threatened yourself. Self knowledge and acceptance are critical factors for leadership since the mission of the leader is to serve others. You must serve without regard for personal preferences. You simply must be clear about who you are and why you are there.

N **Networking human potential.** This is an awesome benefit to volunteerism. Great people will tell you that volunteerism has provided the spring board to their greatest achievements because it is through volunteerism that access to other influential and other interesting people is possible. We will cover this more in the next chapter.

T **Test yourself, help others.** It is often said that no person is an island and this means that no one can expect to operate independently of others in society. What better way to test your skills than by helping others. The real reward is in the "helping." In my mind, the true measurement of maturity is when you gain as much gratification in serving others as you do in serving your self.

E **Educate, Endure, Enjoy.** Great scholars have reached an astounding conclusion. The greatest skill is the skill to learn. To transfer the ability to learn to in new arenas, new times, and new tasks. America is truly poised to learn, to do, and to teach.

This process will teach you to endure while enjoying the sweet victory of accomplishment.

E **Encourage the heart.** Volunteerism is the ideal vehicle to test drive your capabilities. To give all that is within you without regard for a job description. It allows you to display your competencies as a labor of love thereby providing its own reward.

R **Return gift to universe.** It is my belief that when we are born, we are given a gift. How we develop that gift is up to us. While on earth, we are a series of thoughts, ideas, feelings and actions. If we are lucky, we can make our gift our livelihood. To enrich the lives of others, we can contribute our gift to volunteer causes. Each of us has a unique gift of contribution. What we deposit in the universe enables others to determine, develop, and deposit these gifts. Volunteerism provides a controlled vehicle to do this.

As a volunteer, we are able to make our unique contribution by sharing ourselves. What we find is that we can not make a deposit without receiving a return. I encourage you to take a look at yourself where you are, as well as where you want to be.

Achieving universal appeal requires an investment. The returns will not always be evident. Volunteerism is an excellent vehicle to "test drive" your personal drive as you delve into new arenas. It is an excellent opportunity for reflection.

If you are totally satisfied. I applaud you, if not, I suggest that you continue to explore your level of leadership and your level of involvement in the community in which you live and work. It is clear that the line between organizations and communities is starting to blur. Companies are starting to partnership with the community as a sensible business strategy. Your involvement in the community could very well be your springboard to success within your organization.

As we continue to experience the challenges of change, the need to grow, to learn and to earn in non-traditional ways, volunteerism will continue to be a strategy of wisdom and an agenda item on the personal and professional programs of progressive people.

Leadership development and volunteerism are inseparable. Know it and get involved. If you are already involved and have found this chapter to be a reenforcement, I offer my congratulations. More power to you wherever you are making your contributions. It does not matter where you are serving, you are in the right place at the right time, and as only you know, for the right reasons.

Volunteerism is truly a training ground for leadership development and a grand step toward universal appeal.

The largest challenge we have is self mastery as we strive to develop interpersonal relationships with others. Some of our fellow volunteers we will like, some we will not like. Maturity is over-riding personal likes and dislikes for the good of the whole. You can only do this as you work with a variety of people in a variety to situations. We must master our self first, and then others.

It has been my experience that volunteerism extracts a depth of leadership like no other assignment. You work with people that you do not like for reasons that are not evident. You learn to appreciate what they bring to the project rather than who they are. You learn to rise above yourself for a greater cause.

More importantly, you gain the opportunity to look at people as potential. You don't always have the luxury of being choosy. Often you are surprised at how wonderful people are and how wonderful you become when you start to look at people objectively and with positive expectations. You learn the true value of universal appeal as you learn to compromise, to grow, and to succeed—together.

CHAPTER VIII

NETWORKING:

Maximizing Human Potential The Ultimate Case Study For Learning

In years past, organizations spent a lot of time recruiting, selecting, training and developing people. It was felt that the upfront investment would yield long-term results. That was then, this is now.

Organizations still need the people. They must still recruit and select. Training and development of the individual is vastly becoming the responsibility of the individual. Not only must the individual self develop—s/he must self develop with universal appeal.

Instead of recruiting and selecting "potential," organizations are recruiting developed potential. In short, they are attempting to "buy" talent. To put it mildly, they are attempting to buy "refined potential."

It is common knowledge that technical competence is relatively easy to measure. A critical review of credentials, a chat with references, or a few "what if" questions can usually give some insight as to competence. However, compatibility is the primary focal point these days. How will this new talent merge with the existing talent? In many cases, the existing talent is a combination of talent from different sources. The effectiveness of the total is dependent on producing results with other people. "Is s/he a team player?" Will having this person on the team enhance the productivity of the other members while delivering his/her own unique contribution? These are usually the questions.

The skill of developing interpersonal relationships is a primary factor in the success of the individual as well as the organization. It is unlikely that any person will operate as an island. In many cases, there will be numerous islands as companies move to create "entrepreneurial pockets" in an effort to be competitive as a whole. The dual capability of independence and interdependence is not negotiable. The last thing to be tolerated is unhealthy tension. It is a deterrent to productivity, group morale, and the quality of output.

In his book *Moments of Truth,* Juan Carlson talked about the success of organizations being nothing more than "moments of truth." He said that "each time a company comes into contact with your organization in any way, shape form or fashion, they formulate an opinion of your organization." In reality, it is the people and the attitudes of the people that determine the outcome of any transaction.

It has been discovered many times that turnover in organizations is oftentimes related to people rather than products. That is unfortunate and in these competitive times, it is unacceptable. We must develop tolerance for others and of ourselves and our moods. We must learn to master our moods in order to master the ability to develop relationships.

Unlike a definable skill like selling, etc., relationship building is as ongoing as the people that you meet. We are always under construction when it comes to the building of relationships.

In addition to building relationships, we must identify ready resources of information, people, and solutions (IPS). As we emerge deeper into the information age, only information will move us from one level to the next. We must not ask "how", we must ask "who."

If we were going to coin a formula for success, it would be: R + IPS = S.

Relationships plus information, people, and solutions equals success. The achievement of this formula is most easily accomplished through networking.

Networking is nothing more than maximizing human potential.

NETWORKING IS FUN-CTIONAL— NOT JUST FUN

It is not only what you know, or who you know—it is who knows you.

For years, I have made speeches, presented workshops, and made as my personal philosophy the need to network. I have literally preached the need for self promotion in the well orchestrated plan of building visibility. Too many people spend too much time getting good and too little time getting known. As a result, less deserving people end up with the rewards and the hard-working people end up with the reasons. The reasons why they did not get the reward.

In many cases, the self promoting networker will have utilized information retrieved from the hard worker to further his or her cause. While it is unfair, it is not illegal or unusual. It is a classic case of intent not being reconciled with impact. No one is compensated for good intentions, the focus is on results.

This is evident all over the world. This is particularly evident in the government sector as they are literally attempting to "reinvent government." The details of this struggle are outlined in the book *Reinventing Government* by David Osborne and Ted Gaebler. The focus is on results and moving new realities into old institutions. We are clearly faced with the challenge of "teaching old dogs new tricks."

As we move deeper and deeper into the concept of a global marketplace, the ability to meet, recruit, and interact with a diverse group of people will be at the forefront of all skills needed. How do you learn this retroactively? Is there a "crash" course? The answers are that you cannot learn this retroactively—you must start from where you are right now. And No, there is no "crash" course only a sensible solution: Networking.

If you are sincere and sensible, the decision to network will pay big dividends in achieving the formula of R + IPS = S. First of all, networking is fun. It is usually a plan or an unplanned meeting of groups or individuals with the expressed purpose of "mutual gratification." The emphasis is on "mutual."

Because it is planned and the part of a master plan, no effort or insight is lost.

Networking becomes the "ultimate case study for learning." You will learn about yourself and you will learn how you respond to others. You will learn others response to you. These lessons will direct you to a celebration if others respond to you positively. Or a major wake up call if the response is not so positive. You will be naturally guided to the next step.

In the achievement of mastering the Diversity equation, networking is absolutely essential as indicated in our discussion on volunteerism. Unlike volunteerism, networking will not necessarily have as its guide a common project. It may lead to volunteerism, however it is not necessarily the outcome desired. Through volunteerism, transferable *technical* skills are often eminent. Through networking, transferable *interactive* skills will be eminent. We need them both. They can be viewed as a product (technical skills) and a carrier (interactive skills).

In your work as a volunteer, you will generally find people acquiescing to you in order to gain your contributions. It is also eminent in volunteering that as a group you will draw upon the collective talents, experiences, and resources to achieve a common goal. In your pursuit of networking, you will be acquiescing in order to gain access to others. It will depend heavily upon your ability to manage your behavior, what you say and do, to encourage the positive responses of others. In many cases, gaining the endorsement of others will be the ultimate outcome.

It is critical to remember in today's competitive times: "it is not only what you know or even who you know, it is who knows you and who knows what you know."

CHAPTER IX

PERCEPTIONS, PERFORMANCE, AND POWER:

Undisputed Components of Success

While a crisp definition of success is often debated, most people agree that it means something different for each person. It is my belief that the hierarchy of success follows closely the hierarchy of needs according to Maslow.

What is not in dispute are the components of success. Perceptions, Performance, and Power are elements that must be present if one is to gain his/her heart's desire.

To fail at *creating* the proper *perceptions* is to fail at gaining the opportunity to *perform*. Without tangible demonstration of your abilities, there is no way to gain the power of anything. Power is the perception of others that you have something that they need and that it cannot be gained from anyone else.

These factors are hopelessly linked together. Unless enough genius is present to "crash perform" without the consent of others, everything else is blocked.

To ensure that we are all on the same wave length, I will define these three factors:

PERCEPTIONS
Looking good through the eyes of others without regard for what should or should not be.

PERFORMANCE
Being good by any and all standards.

POWER
Making good things happen—your way.

Let's examine each of these individually.

PERCEPTIONS

Joseph P. Kennedy, the father of President John F. Kennedy once said that:

> *It does not matter what you are, what matters is what people think you are.*

While the reality of this is to many people, repulsive, I have found it to be true.

Many people have experienced untold joy/pain; not because they deserved it but because someone thought that they deserved it. This was revealed in an old song by Sam Cook called *"Frankie and Johnny."* As the story goes, Frankie observed Johnny sitting in a bar with another woman. In a fit of jealous rage, she produced a gun an shot Johnny. In his last dying breath, Johnny reveals that he was telling the other woman about Frankie. As he dies, he declares that he loves her. The song ends.

While it is not known whether the song is fact or fiction, the reality is that these things happen every day. Careers die, marriages die, hope dies—all because someone perceived one thing and acted on that perception.

The same is true when people meet for the first time. Each reacts to the other based on what they think they know about each other. In the Diversity equation, sometimes that reaction is based on nothing other than stereotypical rhetoric. If the person(s) with the rhetoric is in the position to give or to withhold opportunity, it is probably withheld. This was demonstrated in the 60 Minutes example where a high ranking official maintained stereotypical views about African-Americans. As a result, suppression of opportunity was running rampant. It ended up on 60 Minutes for the nation to see. It was followed up by a public apology.

The Realities Of Perceptions

- They may or may not be true

- They are used to make decisions

- They are subject to inaccuracy

- They weigh heavily in personnel decisions

- They are used as the basis for evaluating potential

Managing Perceptions

It is my recommendation that you not get into a position of whether or not someone has the right to perceive you inaccurately. I recommend that you make the decision to manage the perception that people have of you without regard for anything other than ensuring that what is perceived is right and reconciled with reality.

I can recall years ago after being recently transferred to a new job. I sensed that the Branch Manager was unusually cool with me but I could not figure out why since I had had no previous experience with him.

Finally, I requested an executive interview. During the interview, I asked him for feedback. He immediately informed me that he felt that I was indecisive. (I am anything but indecisive.) When I asked how he arrived at that conclusion, he related something that was inaccurate regarding my transfer to his branch. In the rush to accommodate my transfer, he had been given only a partial explanation as to why I was coming in one position instead of the one he expected. (The first was communicated without my input, consent, or knowledge.) As a result, he felt that I had put him in a precarious situation and naturally, he resented it.

Had I not acted on my instincts, he would have continued to hold me accountable for something that was not my fault. The results could have been fatal. Instead, he apologized and complimented me on my observations, assertiveness, and my performance.

Here are some suggestions for managing perceptions.

1. Help others to help you. Humility is a powerful tool.

2. Test the reality of your observations. Pan paranoia.

3. Seek feedback from those worthy of giving it. (Peers, superior, etc.)

4. Ask for advice on what you can do to enhance positive perceptions.

5. Be dogmatic in seeking feedback on performance, style, or others perception of you based on this person's observations.

6. Weigh the feedback you receive. Act on it. Assimilate or discount.

7. Give credit to those giving feedback.

While the example I presented was clearly one of superior/subordinate, the same holds true for any relationship worthy of survival. This is particularly true in the Diversity equation if maximum interaction is to be achieved.

Remember Maslow's Hierarchy. If a person perceives that you are "challenging their very right to be there," it is unlikely that you will ever achieve the totality of their brilliance. They will always be guarded and suspicious of your inquiries, information, and integrity.

When one's self image is threatened, productivity will always be less than optimum.

PERFORMANCE

In years past, productivity was defined, visible, measurable and objective. That was then—this is now.

Walter Wriston in his book *The Twilight of Sovereignty* says this:

> *The acceleration toward a global economy has produced a fundamental change in the world's work. The driving force behind that change is information technology and in particular the relative importance of intellectual capital in relation to physical capital. Intellectual capital— human intelligence—is now the dominant factor of production, and the world's most fundamentally important market is the market for intellectual capital. pg. 78*

Managing the Diversity equation is now the pathway to productivity if intellectual capital is important. To think is to produce.

Even when tangible and measurable performance was the key ingredient, there was always an intangible aspect. This presented itself as: attitude, quality, commitment, etc. However, the employee could always appeal based on tangible output. Now the job is to think. In many cases, the thinking is done from a home office. Sometimes the thinking is just part of a functional whole. Intellectual capital is just that—intellect.

If we have had major challenges in the workplace already when the performance was evident, imagine what is going to happen when it is not evident or visible. You cannot sensibly measure brainwaves. Even if you did, you can't determine the content about the activity. And it is clear—one can only effectively think about one thing at a time.

Mr. Wriston says:

The most mobile of all forms of capital will be increasingly intolerant of nationalist restrictions because it will be inherently global and almost immune from nationalist restrictions. Far more than any other form of capital, intellectual capital will go where it is wanted, stay where it is well treated, and multiply where it is allowed to earn the greatest return. pg. 78

This is a sobering reality.

For the first time in my lifetime, the need for mutual respect and integrity is needed to achieve mutual gratification. Performance will clearly be measured by ideas and the successful implementation of those ideas. Once the idea is shared, it can not be retrieved. However, the brain that conceived the idea is still powered up. It will only move to the next idea when the first idea is properly rewarded. If it is not properly rewarded, future ideas will be suppressed, hoarded, or redirected. Self preservation is the first law of nature.

POWER

The business world has changed. Increased competition, domestic and global, has changed the rules . . . Knowing how to exert influence at every level—in your company, in the community, with government, and with the public at large—will spell the difference between success and mediocrity.

Robert L. Dilenschneider
President and CEO
Hill and Knowlton

Power has to be the most intriguing word I have ever spoken. It is a word that people shun out of fear, misunderstanding, and the lack of it. Becoming more comfortable with Power is the pathway to freedom since influence and persuasion are tools of victory.

Power is exercised by either presenting or withholding something that causes others to act in a way even if they are opposed to it. The reality of power says that you must have something someone wants and they must perceive that they can not get it elsewhere.

The simple fact is, the more dependent people are on you and what you can provide to satisfy their needs, the more power you will have. You can only determine the impact of power by occasionally using it. And while you render power counter productive if you overuse it, it is not power if you never use it. Awareness is the key.

In today's times, when information is power, more and more people are figuring out that they have it. It is like a gun. Properly registered and used responsibly, it is a source of power and protection. Improperly registered and used irresponsibly, it becomes a threat.

As people become more and more aware of the power of the brain and why this power must be fed, companies will profit by having organizations that are intellectually superior. However, the flip side of that is that it is like having "power on wheels." As long as people feel respected and valued, they will roll along within the confines of the organization. When they feel disrespected and under-valued, they will simply roll outside of the confines of the organization carrying with them countless scores of information and investments in human capital.

On the other hand, if the employee does not invest enough in his or her own development, chances are they will be rolled out of the organization.

Perception, Performance and Power are intermingled like never before. The real test of power on the part of the employer or the employee will be determined by the number of firms left standing after the shake-outs have been completed.

The interesting and most captivating reality is that now the acquisition and the dissemination of power is a mutual process. It behooves all parties to respect and to respond to the needs of the other. It is clearly two sides of the same coin.

QUESTIONS ABOUT THIS CHAPTER

1. What is your initial reaction to the foregoing?

2. Does it compare to what you have experienced?

3. What have you observed in the workplace that would contradict or confirm the foregoing?

4. What would you add to the chapter you have just read?

5. What do you see as potential solutions?

Recommendation: Choose a person or a group of persons of different gender, culture, race, etc. and initiate a discussion with the intent being:

1. Enlightenment.

2. Developing a functional action plan personally.

3. Exploring the possibilities of developing a functional action plan for the immediate work area.

CHAPTER X

AMERICA'S MOST POWERFUL WEAPON:

Universal Appeal

It is clear that due to all of the turmoil, we must all begin to see ambiguity as a condition of survival and not as a source of confusion. The antidote for confusion is dialogue and we must keep the dialogue open and honest.

THE CHANGING OF THE GUARD

The world can be viewed as going through somewhat of a "changing of the guard." What was being guarded are old concepts created for a time and place that is no longer here. What is being guarded is the status quo. What is being guarded is pride, comfort, and a sense of direction. It is to no avail—it has all changed.

The guard is changing and what was being guarded is changing also. New leaders are emerging. These are young leaders, old leaders, black leaders, female leaders, leaders of different sexual orientation, leaders with disabilities. The day is finally here when what is needed to be in a leadership position is simply to have access to information, to be able to interpret that information, to be able to convert that information into a potential solution, and to assume the position of leadership. We are experiencing a real changing of the guard—we are only missing the official ceremony.

In his book, *Changing of the Guard: Power and Leadership in America*, David S. Broder had these observations about the changing of the guard ceremony:

> *The changing of the guard is a ceremony as old as civilization, and one that is subject to endless rehearsal and repetition. But for each shift, the reality is unambiguous, and it is unique. One moment they are at rest, spectators on the sideline of history. And the next, they are maintaining the guard on which the security of our future depends. pg 468.*

Mr. Broder has defined what many know as simple. There is a time for learning and there is a time for leading. These are both choices. Each person with the responsibility of standing guard knows that to earn the right, they must practice continually. They must preserve the quality of their equipment and focus on a meticulous appearance. This is a continual learning experience. However when it is time to guard, the learning is over and the leading is a requirement.

While there are different requirements for choosing the designated guards, they must all come from the human race. The human race is comprised of people of different origins. While we each have the choice of leading or not leading, what is not a choice is the source of learner, we all arrived in the world the same way—as a world and as individuals, we simply emerge.

We have no input into the decision of evolution. One moment we are non-existent, the next moment we are conceived, and the next thing we know—slap on the rear end. Welcome to the world! If we are lucky, someone will nurture us until we are capable of nurturing ourselves. And then we discover that we have a mind to think and a body to back up our thinking. At this point we become constructive to society or destructive to society.

We quickly learn that we are operating with and against others who arrived the same way that we did. We learn that what we think or do not think will determine how we feel. How we feel determines what we do. What we do or do not do, will determine the outcome of our dreams.

Unfortunately, we also learn that many times, others too, are working to have input into our thoughts and our actions. Sometimes this input is positive and sometimes it is not.

We also learn that it is in the thinking, that some people decide that they are superior to others. Driven by that belief, they work to declare certain groups "outcasts." They work to exclude them from impacting decisions affecting the very world we live in.

While I have personally been the object of discrimination many times, I have never been able to figure it out. What is it that makes these people feel that they or anyone else have more of a right to exist or to lead than anyone else? After all, none of us had any input into when we arrived. We had absolutely no input into how we looked, etc.

Many of the perpetrators of discrimination actually hate the way they look and in many cases, they hate the way they are. Certainly, if they had any power to determine the evolution of man, they would have altered their own existence. Yet, day after day, they perpetuate the myth of superiority without regard for reality. I still find it perplexing but unworthy of respect.

EXCUSE ME, THAT'S MY LIFE

Finally, people of all races, sexes, etc. are waking up to the fact that we are all equal. Yes, we look different and in many cases we are different. This is what makes the world a world. What makes us unique is how we fold our contributions into the overall genius of mankind and remain unique. It is finally apparent to *all of us* that *no one of us* has the power to determine the fate of *any of us.*

Like the election process, we all have one vote or one life. If we want the power of other votes, then we must influence the custodians of other votes. Finally, the oppressed are saying: "excuse me, that's my life." We recognize that the guard is changing and we are up next if we choose to take a stand.

Michael Korda in his book: *Power, How To Get It—How To Use It,* written in 1974, re-wrote the Preface for the 1990's. He writes that in the 1970's

> *it was scandalous to suggest that in the real world people form pecking orders, that some people will always in any organization, try to bully and intimidate others, that the world is not necessarily a nice place, and that the only person who is going to look out for you is you yourself. Well the world has changed since then. . . . pg ix*

People of all disciplines are rising up against anyone who would trespass on their freedom or the freedom of others. They are recognizing and declaring that they have contributions to make and they are making them. They are learning the power of perception, performance, and power. As they learn the power of influence, they too are becoming contributing leaders. They are taking their seat at the table.

Many already at the table are simply sliding over and saying welcome, may I pass you the *power.* Some are offering resistance. This means that their efforts are diverted from the *"war"* to the *"battle."* In many cases they are being invited away from the table because in the battle of competition and customer retention, there is no place for anyone who does not understand the war of survival. They do not understand that the fatalities of battle creates weaknesses in the struggle of war. We need leadership, team players, and dogged determination to win—there is no time or respect for discrimination.

David Broder expressed his glee at the outcome of this reality when he said:

Nothing touched me more in all the interviewing than the stories of those people who have moved in their own lifetime from being outcasts of this society to being contributing leaders. pg 470

THE WIDENING OF THE LEADERSHIP POOL

The cry for leadership is loud. Leadership in every shape of the word is needed if we are to navigate ourselves out of the emerging confusion that has overtaken the world.

Everything in our world is under siege. The family structure is being threatened, the children are rising up and taking a fatal approach to conflict resolution—which oftentimes result in death. The church is being challenged, the political structure and all of its leaders are being challenged. Businesses are being forced to respond to Wall Street instead of the needs of its people, and the beat goes on. . . . Everyone with an eye and a brain is needed. We are all watchdogs for change and truant officers in search of solutions.

We don't have time to fight each other anymore. We have a world to save. As a country, we must regain our rightful place as "the number one superpower." I just don't believe that any country that set the pace for all other countries, must get in line. If information is power, then we are the superpower. We must demonstrate that again.

As a superpower we created the pathway of entry for many different groups. They came, they saw, they learned the rules, and now they want to play. They are playing and playing well. In some cases, they are out playing us. Our only challenge is amassing the input of all of the members of the new and diverse American team. We must adapt a sports mentality. We must develop a strategy, choose our players, and play this game to win. We simply must gain and maintain "a level playing field."

Like in sports, our only focus should be on who can get the ball across the goal line. Skills, talent, wit, leverage, energy, and enthusiasm. These things are race and gender neutral. Our approach should be also.

Changing of the Guard: Power and Leadership In America was copyrighted in 1980. David S. Broder made certain predictions and observations. I find them quite accurate and still emerging. He was very clear about the dilemma of discrimination and its impact on leadership resources as it is eradicated. He had this to say:

> *The success in the past twenty years of the struggle against discrimination is beginning, like the investment in education, to repay us rich rewards in the widening of the leadership pool. It is remarkable to think that in 1960 no Catholic had ever served as President, no black had served in the Cabinet or on the Supreme Court, and both Hispanics and women were notable by their absence in decision-making posts.*

> *All of the groups are still under-represented in our leadership. But having won major battles against the legal and social barriers blocking them from the mainstream of American life, they are coming on—and fast.*

> *There is no way to know who specifically will be running this country in 1990 or 2000, but it is certain that the*

leaders will have a vastly different look—a far greater mixture of races, religions and sexes—than they have today.

And a good thing, too—not simply because it will make us feel better about ourselves, and make our government more representative than it has been. The simple fact is that when everybody competes, and not just male white Protestants, the people who emerge with power have to be that much better equipped to do their jobs. pg 470

I reiterate at this point that I do not believe that the shrinking of white male presence is the total answer. I do not believe that it is even a partial answer. The focus should not be in shrinking one group to enlarge another. It should be to ensure that each group is given the opportunity to contribute in a meaningful and a relevant way. I think that a society *absent* of white male input is as bad as a society with *only* white male input. It is not a total society. We must cease with the devisive thinking. We must think inclusion and collaboration.

I concur with Mr. Broder when he says that a leader with the responsibility of leading a diverse following will just get better as a leader. We could, in fact call it, universal leadership.

America is in a war, a war of survival.

In my mind it is a massive ground attack on all fronts. The weapons are different than in traditional wars—these are intellectual weapons. Intellectual capital comes in many strengths, colors, and sexes. It is transferable and capital will always seek its most productive use. The mind, like the body gets stronger and better as we use it in productive and constructive ways. We must use the intellectual weapons that are housed in this great country to enable us to shake hands with other great countries. This is no longer negotiable. Diversity is our greatest weapon. It is our strongest asset.

THE WALLS MUST COME DOWN

John Linder, Member of Congress representing the 4th District of Georgia, in his defense of the North American Free Trade Agreement (NAFTA), wrote:

> Whether we like it or not, we live in a global economy. People cross national boundaries as easily as our grandparents crossed from state to state. We simply cannot leave walls between nations whose people want nothing more than increased trade among friends . . .
>
> NAFTA is not a jobs program or an economic booster shot. It is a foreign policy initiative between two peoples who have moved closer together in interests and aspirations and who desire to remove the barriers that artificially separate their entrepreneurs from our entrepreneurs. The walls should come down.

While the House of Representatives voted to pass NAFTA by a vote of 234 to 200 on November 17, 1993, one cannot ignore the separation of minds on what will surely change the face of the way we do business in the world. To me, it means that 200 people or 200 votes were against and 234 were for NAFTA. Will we come together now that the majority has spoken?

This is indicative of the battle that sometimes goes on in the workplace. The major difference being Diversity instead of NAFTA. The majority is responding positively to the Diversity in the workforce and a great many are responding negatively to it. If that is the case, we are in for a major upset.

We have not resolved our *internal* struggle within our domestic realms and now we are taking on the world. To me, it is like trying to run a race with your pants around your knees. Truly, we will rise and fall many times before someone declares a winner. Unless we can call a permanent cease-fire, the winner will not be America. It has been said many times, "a house divided against itself will not stand." We are all in this foxhole together.

The walls must come down within our internal infrastructure just as they must come down from geographic boundaries. We have many weapons in America, but the best weapon is being fired with a "silencer." It is time to fire a shot of togetherness so that the shot will be heard around the world.

One team, many talents, one goal. The goal is to win. Universal Appeal is America's Most Powerful Weapon.

QUESTIONS ABOUT THIS CHAPTER

1. What is your initial reaction to the foregoing?

2. Does it compare to what you have experienced?

3. What have you observed in the workplace that would contradict or confirm the foregoing?

4. What would you add to the chapter you have just read?

5. What do you see as potential solutions?

Recommendation: Choose a person or a group of persons of different gender, culture, race, etc. and initiate a discussion with the intent being:

1. Enlightenment.

2. Developing a functional action plan personally.

3. Exploring the possibilities of developing a functional action plan for the immediate work area.

CHAPTER XI

WHERE DO WE GO FROM HERE?

I have shared with you what we need to do. I have shared with you why we need to do it. I would be remiss if I did not offer input and suggestions on how to do what we need to do.

Diversity is reality. Managing the reality of Diversity is a decision. It is as much a personal decision as it is a business decision. Training sessions, awareness sessions, counseling, and all of societies approaches will do nothing until you as an individual have decided to change the way you look at the issue. Once that decision is made, then and only then will the desire to be effective in this process lead you to the right answers for you.

A good case an point is my rejection of raw oysters for years. I could not conceive of anything more grotesque than eating something without cooking it. In my mind, it was barbaric and of the cave man mentality. I felt that oysters were to be deep fried in a light batter or at the very least, dropped in seafood gumbo to add flavor.

Finally, a few years ago, I was on a business boat ride. As usual, the delicacy was raw oysters. One of my colleagues observed my horror as I observed him indulging and made it his appointed duty to have me at least try one. He appealed to my "risk taker" nature, etc. After dipping the oyster into a flavorful sauce, I held my breath and tried it. To my surprise, it was not distasteful at all; in fact, it was very tasty. My concern was that it slid down my throat before I could savor the taste.

Do I eat raw oysters today? No. I still do not choose them, however, I do have an appreciation for those that do. My compromise is to eat "Oysters Rockerfeller." I still get the ambiance of the shell, it is not deep fried, and it gives me a flavor that I can savor for a while.

My favorite slogan is "don't knock it until you have tried it." It is a persuasive response to unjustified resistance. That is my message to you if you have been resisting the "dawning of diversity."

Ivory Dorsey

Don't, I beg of you, do not force yourself to tolerate people or things that are obviously in conflict with your value system. You will find as I have that there will be many things and many people who will turn you off. I ask you to not be hasty in judgment. Do not be stereotypical. Make sure that it is the behavior of the person, not the culture, the race, the gender, etc.

Aside from the obvious business benefits, a tolerance for Diversity enriches your life. It expands your sphere of life. It provides personal and professional etching that a one dimensional life simply cannot provide.

Where we go from here is to decide. Then we must develop the desire.

HOW DO WE GET STARTED? AN INTERNAL PACKAGE CALLED DESIRE

1. **Decide to delve into the differences in others.** Do not be timid about this. When you have met someone and have developed a working relationship with them, be open about your desire to know more about them. Express the fact that the "obvious" differences in sex, race, culture, physical capability, sexual orientation, etc. has elevated your curiosity. Explain that you feel that reconciling what you know about them and what you do not know is important to you. If you are sincere, this will be well received.

I can recall being friends with a male who was, at the time bisexual. We spent a lot of time together and respected each other both personally and professionally. Finally, one day he asked me to go to lunch with him. He said that he had something very important to discuss with me. I was very concerned and immediately agreed to accommodate him. He insisted on picking me up and driving to the designated place.

Once I was in the car, he launched into what was obviously a very painful discussion. He explained that he had been holding something back from me and he felt that it was impeding the flow of our relationship. I could not imagine what it was. He was a white male and he was Jewish; there was a lot that I did not know about both of these things so I was quite curious.

Finally, he said that he was "bisexual." He went on to explain that though he had been married before, he considered himself to be bisexual. He looked at me and waited for what he thought would be a shocked or negative response. I started to laugh hysterically. My laughing did not set well with him because he assumed that I was laughing at what he had said.

I was laughing because I already suspected that he was not bisexual but outright gay. History has proven that to be a fact since later that same year, he reached the same conclusion and took on a permanent male "significant other." When I explained to him why I was laughing, he too, started to laugh. He asked me how long had I known and how did I feel about it? I told him that I had suspected immediately because of the way he carried himself. In addition to my own observations, others had told me he was gay in an effort to influence me to avoid him.

How did I feel about it? I did not care one way or the other since I had no romantic interest in him personally. What I liked about him was his obvious intelligence, his sensitivity, his sense of humor, his broad knowledge about business, and the list goes on.

While I did not harbor any hostilities about his sexual preference, I was curious about how he felt that it impacted him. I was also curious as to how he felt it would impact the quality of our future relationship. I had many questions and he was more than happy to oblige me with the answers. He is now one of my closest associates.

2. **We must develop empathy to understand others.** We must put ourselves in the place of others. It was the only way I was able to develop a working relationship with my white male counterparts when I took on my first management job. I had to ask myself the question: "how would I feel if I were a white male in a company that obviously respected and complied with Affirmative Action and Equal Opportunity and a high performing Black Woman was put on a team of all white males?"

Would I be experiencing anxieties? Would I suspect that soon she would be my boss? Would I instinctively decide to "kill her before she multiplies?" Would I approach her, or would I wait to see if she wanted to be approached? Once I put myself in their places, I understood better that it was my responsibility to create a climate for understanding and support. The fact is at that level, a certain amount of tension is present anyway because of the need to balance competition and cooperation—what a paradox? Empathy is a powerful tool to understanding.

3. **Sincerity cannot be faked.** If you are sincere in your approach, there is very little that can go wrong. As humans, we have instincts and we know when people are wholesaling sincerity and when it is customized. Sincerity starts in the mind, the thought process and moves to behavior. Finally, after much work, it moves to the heart. Emotions follow logic, not the other way around.

4. **Initiate the approach.** My gay friend recognized a need to communicate more freely. He took the risk that he might be rejected. We all loathe rejection. Take the risk to initiate action. The other person is as nervous as you are, in many cases, they will since your sincerity and meet you half way.

5. **When someone does initiate the approach,** respond openly. Acknowledge your glee that they felt comfortable enough to approach you. Acknowledge that this is tough for all of us. Do not be critical if the person is not "politically correct" in their semantics. If an older person refers to you as "colored or negro," know that they are operating from where they are. It is your responsibility and your privilege to take them to the next level. Take the high road.

I can recall meeting my neighbor's new wife. They are both from Kentucky and they are lovely people. When she first arrived in July, she would refer to me as "colored." Her husband's birthday is January 15, to me, the significance of that date is that is Martin Luther King, Jr.'s birthday.

On his first birthday, six months after they were married, she had a party and invited me. I waited for a light moment and I said to him, *"for your birthday, I want your wife to stop calling me colored."* Everyone laughed, including her though she was obviously confused, well why not call me colored. He being an executive in a leading company explained. At that time, she explained that she never saw a "black" person until she was 16 years old, etc.

This also opened the door for other discussion. The relationship was strengthened.

Of course, after that, Jessie Jackson announced that we are not "Black," we are African-American. Not only am I not going to saddle her with that, I am not going to deal with it either. I use "Black" and "African-American" interchangeably

For God's sake, do not penalize people for what they do not know. Open up your heart. The world is getting so complicated that it is hard to keep up with the changes. It is as if once we learned all of the answers, someone changed the questions. Let's relax and live. Let's stop taking ourselves so seriously. Life is too short and things are really getting exciting now. Let's join forces, buckle up, and enjoy the ride!

6. **Enjoyment** is the reward of Diversity. It is a joy to eat lunch with people who are different from you. It is a real blast to openly point out the different perspectives and to laugh about them. It is wonderful to experience concerns about perceived differences and have the wherewithal to explore the perceptions. Have a laugh. Have a life.

Periodically, I have lunch with a white male lawyer friend of mine. He is quite established economically and on this day, I decided to take him to a Black-owned and operated restaurant. In getting there, we had to travel on a one-way street. Since I was unfamiliar with the location, I inadvertently passed the entry. I yelled my dismay because to get into the place, I had to go around the block. He looked bewildered, he looked back and observed that no one was behind us and asked: "won't this car go in reverse?"

I looked at him, put the car in reverse, and the rest is history. I immediately said to him—"that was white male behavior, you guys don't follow rules, you just make them!" We both laughed hysterically and had a great lunch.

Diversity is the Garden of life—enjoy.

For your convenience and use, I have created a summary of this. On the next page a sheet entitled: **"DIVERSITY: HOW DO WE GET STARTED? AN INTERNAL PACKAGE CALLED DESIRE."** Copy this sheet, place it in strategic places, remember to refer to it and go out and explore the differences. Remember that it is the differences that make the difference.

DIVERSITY: HOW DO WE GET STARTED?

An *Internal Package* Called *Desire*

D   **D**ecide to delve into the differences in others.

E   **E**mpathy for others is critical for understanding.

S   **S**incerity in your approach is imperative.

I   **I**nitiating the approach is helpful.

R   **R**esponsiveness when approached is key.

E   **E**njoyment is the reward.

Note: The most important ingredient is sincerity. A genuine desire to recognize, to understand, to respect, and to appreciate the differences; this is all that can be expected. Once this is achieved, you will know what to do next.

You will find that though there *are* differences, it is the "differences" that make the *difference* in achieving optimum performance.